The Beautiful Perfect Seven

J. Clement Phillips

Published in the USA by:
Harvest Seed Books
P.O. Box 493557
Redding, CA 96049-3557

ISBN: 978-1-7349860-3-7 Hardback with dust jacket
         978-1-7349860-4-4 Paperback
         978-1-7349860-5-1 (ebook)

Printed in the United States of America

Book & cover design by Darlene & Dan Swanson • www.van-garde.com

To the Beautiful Perfect Seven:

Caleb, Jacob, Autumn, Hannah, Emma, Christian and Abbie.

No words exist to convey my endless love for each of you. I stand humbled and in awe at the majesty of your existence. My thoughts overflow with gratitude. You are greater than great. You are all more than exceptional. Outstanding. Beautiful. Perfect. There is no one who will convince me otherwise.

Disclaimer

THE BEAUTIFUL PERFECT SEVEN IS written from the author's memories which contain some real cracks, cavernous holes and dangerous pitfalls. Sorry, just the way it goes. All names have been avoided on purpose. Any place mentioned comes from best recollection. Memories are a tricky thing. I wrote this from a heart which has some undeniable broken parts, but with openness and as honestly as recollection permits. We all know that human memory is deeply flawed. Deeply may not be the right word. Exceedingly, but this may be a bright light to highlight this personal written journey. I freely overlapped some times and situations on purpose as going too far down the path of years and times threatened to undo me. Please have grace and a sliver of mercy for my shortcomings. I did it on purpose.

The Beautiful Perfect Seven
A Journey

IN THE MIDDLE HALF OF the fifth decade of life I experienced, am still experiencing, a significant and thoroughly uncomfortable alteration in personality, outlook, mindset and philosophy, right to the core of my being. It started with a life change. A down in the dirt shift life alteration. Looking back, it would be easy to proclaim this as a gift, but through the process I will say, I would not wish this on my worst enemy. Well, maybe on my enemy, but miles and an arm's length away from any of those I care about by many multiples, squared.

The best illustration I can give is a string. A little piece of thread sticking out and waiving in the wind attached to the core of my soul. For years, decades, I snipped and chiseled, cut and manicured all the unseemly overgrowth of my troubled soul so it would shine brightly for the sake of my protection and to make others feel less than themselves.

Let me say upfront, this is horrible, worse than horrible, despicable and downright evil and I have no excuse. I am to blame; I fully acknowledge my clear and undeniable part, and I cannot go back. Why would I want to and what would I do?

I lived against my nature with a bright shine and fresh smelling bouquet of pure and undefiled prosperity, which you could take to the bank. In fact, I spent years hidden behind a lie, a plastic mask, keeping my true nature buried as I said yes and amen to any and all requests coming my way. It worked out mostly. The Beautiful, Perfect Seven came into my life. I did not go bankrupt, or go off the deep end until everything settled down and I pulled the string attached to my soul and spun out of control and became undone.

An understatement.

Time became a commodity on my side, or against me as I look back. Either way, I went through a life alteration from making hundreds of decisions daily to a full stop with nothing to do. I sold a business, properties, and went from ultra-high-speed manic living to a tortoise trot all in a matter of days.

Nothing to do anymore.

Left to myself, with nothing or not much to do, gave me the opportunity to reflect and contemplate. Nothing big at first. Only an inventory, observation, and reflective view of my life. As I took time to reflect on my wheelie ways, a shining beam came from nowhere and burst wide open like a spot light of accusation against my very nature. A bright illumination pin-pointing everything, making me up. All the decisions I made, every choice, all the times I said yes, without consideration, or dreamed up a new idea and set my feet to walking, everything all at one time and the most painful regrets filled me to overflowing with a threat to leave me in a ditch mentally naked in despair.

I pulled the wispy, irritating, flapping, nearly invisible fabric attached to my soul, instead of just snipping it away like I did all the other times in my life. I did not pinch the accuser, or tie it in knots down to the marrow and moved on. Nope. Not this time. This time I pulled and pulled and unraveled, turned emotionally inside out, flapping in the wind, exposed and reeling in a bad way. A horrible, grotesque way.

My fault, I take all the blame, but no way to put the genie back in the bottle. I rubbed the glass and the mystical creature materialized with a vengeance. No three wishes and no way to put the cork back, so come what may, and it did in spades. Now I am working to beat back the vicars of death, hell and the grave.

Not an easy task.

The life change, sprinkled by a time of reflection, brought to the surface a clear and undeniable fact of the frailty of my existence, all twisted together as a perfect storm with rumbling quakes shaking my foundation and unleashing a tsunami of havoc. The extreme weather change of life brought about serious destruction, opening up an opportunity to come to grips with who I am, who I have always been. An unwilling participant hidden behind walls of protection I built brick by brick. Then the walls came tumbling down and my mind broke wide open.

Not a pleasant site to see.

They call it a breakdown, mental crack up, going nuts, crazy, insane, the list can go on with more colorful and descriptive phases. Safe to say, I lost my mental grip on reality and snapped. It did not happen in a vacuum or in a single day. Months upon months brought me to the edge of the cliff where mental stability gives way to an endless chasm of darkness in a lifeless abyss.

I did not jump, nor did I fall. I found myself on the aged, but not over the cliff, kicking and screaming all the way. My efforts, manipulative skills, deal making abilities, promises, threats, arrogance, pride, proved less than fruitless and counterproductive.

No one on the planet can say with absolute certainty the reason or purpose. I am not unhappy to come to this revelation. Down deep I somehow knew all of our individual minds hold unattainable depths which is difficult to fully mine, tap into and quantified. I am not bitter at this clear truth, I only held a slight hope when my mind broke to pieces, I might come out on the other side with two fists gripped on the answer holding tightly to deliverance and ultimate freedom. I tried my best, submitted, bent down and gave my whole heart to get help and then I found myself rebuked, deeply wanting, and utterly flabbergasted, left isolated, all alone in a strange dark place.

It is my fault. I believed the educated could help me. I looked across the internet in my home town for experts. It turned out only one Physiatrist provided service in a city of one hundred thousand human beings, plus twice as many in the surrounding communities. WOW! No kidding. But this doctor of mind medicine was not without resources. In fact, he employees dozens and dozens of others to do the work of mental healthcare. From young, debt-stricken graduates with quasi psychology degrees, to physician's assistances (PA), to billing clerks and marketing gurus. A racket I could not keep myself from secretly admiring with a desire to invest, but I restrained myself.

To say I was compulsive might be an understatement. I know I don't have the issues of washing my hands excessively, or counting on my fingers continually or locking doors over and over, but when it comes to finding things out, I have a real problem. I will highlight this in more detail later. Until then, I can only say I let my fingers do the dancing across the "World Wide Web" honed down to find the head shrinks around me and in no time a truth blared with bright red blinking clarity. Mental health is deep, wide and far.

How pitiful, how sad and utterly painful.

In my investigation, I found the one Psychiatrist and countless of other Psychologists. Gobs and gobs right here in river city. Some with Doctoral degrees, meaning they are doctors of the mind, PHD's in mental health issues. Seems good, right? Highly educated, years of passing tests, hundreds of hours of personal talk therapy, perfect. I made a list of twenty-five of these professionals within thirty miles of my home. I reached out to each one of them, which means I called them all to get an appointment for a diagnosis and treatment plan. It did not go as I expected.

Woe to those in need.

Turns out there is an under supply of mental health professionals and an oversupply of crack pots. A sad reality pointing a firm finger of accusation with an uncontested guilty verdict against the whole of our society. Plus, the undisputed fact leaves a chilling, creepy, scary, hidden reality. Where and who are all these people?

Now I know. I am one of them.

Shit.

Many of the mind gurus told me they were full. A few did not call back, and then there were the waiting lists? Crazy people being told they are on a waiting list may be worse than a real-life horror story, in my ignorant whacked out option. I had this weird thought of people across my region with significant mental issues snapping their finger at loved one's saying with real conviction, "GET AWAY FROM THE PHONE, IT MIGHT BE MY APPOINTMENT." As a side note this thought of others almost crippled me, but I placed my thoughts on the Beautiful Perfect Seven and kept a portion of my mind intact, at least outwardly. Internally, I existed as a mush pot between logic, delusion, sanity and bat shit crazy.

Not a good place to exist, by any means.

I went through the landmines set before me and hired the one psychiatrist, and three separate psychologists with two in the wings who asked me to call them back in two months. I am keeping them in my back pocket, just in case.

Through the process, I learned some very helpful and undeniable truths.

One truth seems based in fact. TALK THERAPY takes a long time and does not produce very favorable results. It seems to be a feel-good mechanism with low outcomes. My reasoning for this goes to the infrastructure. Once a week, one-hour sessions over four weeks with the professionals who need many more weeks to come up to speed, reveals the problem. When you go nuts, a month is an eternity.

Trust me.

I came to a clear understanding over a period of frustrating time. I entered into a never-ending maze of dead ends trying to find answers in a flawed system, based on observation, tied to esoteric philosophies and chemical treatment which by all rational scientific confirmation struggle to produce favorable results. Favorable in a twenty percent range. Thank God we do not allow immunizations based on such numbers. "Hey you don't want polio, take this shot, it has a twenty percent chance of success."

Are you kidding me?

This is the way of mental health treatment in this informational and technological age. Far below par, at least from my unstable observation.

Treatments with success rates so lacking would be outlawed anywhere and anyplace, pure and simple, but the big insurance companies pay, or reimburse, for this with millions and millions of dollars. Any sound minded, sober minded, logically thinking human being would shut down such a failing system producing these horrifying results in a split. But no, the system is on the rise with an endless supply of eager and willing lab rats.

I became just another sucker, left wanting with very few options. I knew I needed help, real help, only to find the internet, with shiny websites of PHD's and other head shrinks lacking any actual ability to provide life changing help. I did get accepted into several practices, great name right, "Practice." I paid and bent over to the snake oil sales charlatans for weeks.

Shame on me.

I get it now; this is the way of this highly technical world with highfalutin words, lacking substance when it comes to the science and treatment of mental disorders.

A diagnosis can only come from speculation. What a great science. Observation, maybe a bit of computer algorisms, a few hours of listening with checks in boxes on a sheet based on yes or no and maybe. My first and current philosophy of this pseudoscience turns on the dime and shines with a bright illumination behind bright shadows. "Three-Card Monte," or "The Cup and Balls Shell game." Head shrinks appear to be no better than the carnival pitches asking for a nickel to go behind the flaps of a tent to see the REPTILE CHILD, SORD SWALLER, BEARDED LADY or, well, let your mind fill in the blanks.

Pseudoscience or downright scam?

Instead of a nickel, I use a thin, bright debit card to swipe hundreds of dollars for urine, blood tests and an hour of talking. This is at the one Psychiatrist's, impressive, well organized and professional business. I wanted to say racket, but... The Psychiatrist who owns the place is not the one who you meet with personally. Instead, there is a plethora of paid employees who do the down in the ditch work. I met with a physician's helper. They call themselves a PA's. The PA can work with any specialty. General practitioner, OBGYN, internal medicine, take your pick. After forty-five minutes across a cheap Formica desk, the twenty something PA made a diagnosis. Before they confirmed if I might be a heroin addict, meth smoking lying piece of shit or a true blue out of my mind wacko, two prescriptions were written and placed in my shaky hands.

Am I wrong? How can a physician's assistant, who, by the way, struggled to take my blood pressure, prescribe mind alternating drugs after less than an hour and after checking boxes on a screen? I do not have an answer. Just the way of the world we live in or the underbelly of mental health care treatment.

Looking back, I assume the script; I could fill in at any pharmacy, did not come with the signature of the PA, but contained a copied or facsimile signature of the big dog Psychiatrist who I never talked with. This is a wonderful country, isn't it? Debt infused mid-twenties, paper pushers can write a prescription for mind changing chemicals, after typing on a computer the words I unraveled and left my guts bare for less than an hour, without confirming background, my favorite color, siblings, desires, fears, phobias. Someone must be able to give a high five to my conclusion. Maybe I am wrong. I have been wrong before, many times on countless occasions.

My goal is to take much of my life, spell it all out in utter humiliating detail with no filter as talk therapy in written form here.

Who knows it may have value?

This is one of three parts of my mental health therapy I have embarked on. The other two I will get into later, as I am still refining the end result.

A Journey

In the beginning, right after my crack up, I felt as if I had a clear path. Psychiatrists, and Psychologist, both holding pretentious degrees and pedigrees, living with pats on the shoulders and "that-a-boys" so the uneducated, web savvy designers could create the DOC's or PHD's internet present and sites to look professional and sweet. These head shrink's all have years, maybe decades of schooling.

Seems good, right?

Not.

Instead, I choose to not go down a different path. Three paths, in fact. The first is personal talk therapy in written form. I am hunting and pecking these words out as one part of my treatment. So far, I have found tangible value in this exercise, to open up and unfold my experiences, thoughts, struggles. I have specifically chosen to live in an isolated place with one true and powerful thought. The Beautiful, Perfect Seven. They anchor me, hold me attached to my feet on the ground, and keep my head from spinning out of control. The seven are my refuge in this stormy time as I unfold my heart and squirrelly life. Stay with me as I attempt to expose my soul.

Here goes.

The Struggle and the Lie.

A painful reality I diligently practiced covering up worked and keep buried rose up and exposed me. My heart bursts with a countless supply of brilliant sparks of uncontainable light and at the same time, horrible amounts of hopeless darkness in the depths no scientist can prove exists. I can state unequivocally my reality, which is difficult to quantified, is only one of billions of individual beings who live with countless thoughts and unexplainable feelings.

I am only one.

I have been able to avoid and overlook numerous wild and weird ideas for large swatches of my conscious life, but they caught me with a strangling grip I find myself unable to get free from. I worked my heart out to shut and lock the door, hide the key, and did fairly well until now. Very few of my tricks work any longer, and the floodgate of my hidden thoughts burst from behind the dam I erected. A massive flood rages in torrents I have no control over. All I can do is let it flow and embrace the risk to open up and share.

This is where the Beautiful, Perfect Seven come in. The absolute greatest, most awesome, magnificent seven hold my heart; keep my mind from complete instability as deep-rooted seeds and give me hope.

As a medicine I endeavor to spill my guts, get out the rambling thoughts I allowed to twist my mind and believe the flood will subside and settle down. No way to tell, but worth the possibility. I am not sure where the road will lead or end up, but I have some anticipation most of the crazy in me will find itself left in the dust of typed words. Can't say I have confidence, only a need to try.

I will do my best.

Since my earliest recollection, an overwhelming feeling or understanding, or delusion, of the existence of life pointed a finger of accusation against my sanity. Ever since I can remember, I have difficulty coming to grips with a simple truth everyone I know accepts without question and I understand why, but torment's me to no end. I taught myself, programmed myself, learned to keep far from my mind these thoughts, so I could live like everyone else, to avoid a horrible debilitation which overcomes me, twisting my guts into a tense disabling pretzel with the lie I fought my whole life against, kicking at the door to rush in with guns blaring for one purpose.

Take over and take me out.

I understand this may come across as esoteric and melodramatic, but the struggle is real in me and the lie comes with various weapons I have raised shields against for years, although I have yet to fully extinguish, the power.

First the struggle in a few words, then the lie.

The struggle each of us, all human beings, live inside separate bodies, alone, isolated as biological creatures looking out from the beating shell we live in, move around, taking us where we decide. Step by step as we walk. But we do not move, our bodies take us short distances at a slow rate of speed. If we get into an automobile, we go sustainably faster and farther. On a boat we go leagues, a plane, air miles, and if by space ship, to the cosmos, but those vehicles are not us, just as our body is not who we are, only a container. The place we exist as secluded beings inside a fantastic covering of meat, flesh, bone, blood, and muscle. A weird and fantastic biological organic body with countless nerve endings stimulating gratification or unconscionable pain. This simple truth is a struggle my small mind finds difficulty getting around. So much beyond my ability to comprehend in my miniscule self, but it does not keep me from trying even in the midst of an empty face of vanity.

We all come in different shades, sizes and shapes. A fact no one can deny. None of us have an ability to choose where and how we come into existence. The country, nationality, family or lack thereof, is beyond our choice or decision. Dark skin or pale, thick or thin eyebrows, shapely hips or bony, flabby or skinny, wrinkled, smooth, shiny or blotched, it does not matter. A weird truth and sad issue, as a mighty distraction all human beings struggle through. From inside we look outside, judge, compare, wish, hate, feel better or less then. The external has massive influence. So much beauty out there, so much wonder and so much we have so little control over.

The thought I came into existence from a microscopic seed from one being connected to a tiny egg in another blows my mind. Literally. Plus, as a side note, I split cell by cell, formatted, turned and twisted and grew inside someone else until I sucked in a breath with both freshly configured lungs and then bellowed out a cry. No need to count all the other breaths I have taken since as I take them for granted. I also take for granted the other intricate systems, skeletal, muscular, circulatory, nervous, to name a few, and this is only me as just one of billions of my same species. Then there are so many groups of animals, plants and every other living thing. Hundreds of billions of unique, sophisticated life forms. Many look out of their distinctive coverings as we do, feeling pain, but their language in not human.

This is the struggle my mind tries to contemplate, recognize, understand. I cannot deny the reality of our organic existence, so I mostly overlook and accept facts as they are, even though they are so far behind my ability to wrap my head around. This has proven an effective tool but only keeps the lie dormant, not destroyed.

The Lie

Because of my inability to fathom a never-ending universe, with scientifically proven laws, energy and time, space and light, gravity, seasons, a sadistic lie pops its ugly face into my mind. Sometimes subtle, other times, in a clear fierce attack utilizing mathematical equations, musical theory, history, stories (fact or fiction) with secret messages. A hidden language all pointing a dagger into my heart, to make me dabble with the delusion NOTHING is REAL. I actually exist somewhere else and this world, this life is a training ground until I accept the truth, give in and let go until I am transported to my actual existence far from this overwhelming mind-boggling place. I know this is not true. I know, but I struggle in a deep place, down inside to shake off this terrifying creepy hallucination.

The best way to explain how this lie effects is in the way it starts. From a thought, or a connection of an esoteric message I seemed to hear coming from different places in quick succession. To illustrate, I may hear, out of the blue, by a clerk in a store, a vague reference to one thing or the other. No big deal. Happens all the time to all of us, but somehow, I connect the words to a story I read, which brings a recollection from some historical event, attached to a scene in a movie I saw, triggering the beginnings of the lie. "THE SECRET MESSAGE." I know it sounds weird, but I am beyond concern for appearance. I cannot explain how, only to say, it starts with a subtle rumbling like a soft ethereal familiar wind chime blowing a tune of despair wanting to enter and take up residence with the end result, captivity of my soul. Sometimes I shack my head in fast thrusts back and forth. Other times I speak out load, when no one is there. For some reason, I still have pride or logic or the strong desire to remain outside a lockdown facility. Anyway, the lying chime rings and I put up one of my shields to make it go silent. Interesting enough, the door did not open very often for years, but the knocking comes out of the blue without warning so I stand guard with patient diligence.

I will give a physical comparison as a descriptive understanding which comes, oddly enough, with physical attributes.

At the age of eleven, I had my first of many massive migraine headaches. Horrible pain no med seemed to touch. The thoughts of my eyesight being less than twenty-twenty became the first line of defense. Sure enough, I needed glasses. When I put the spectacles on, I felt quite a bit taller and I have worn them every day of my life since. They did nothing to stop the migraines but I could see all the girls in my school with a new found clarity which leaves me with a lifelong appreciation in the beauty God created.

These painful headaches came around like an unwelcome thief every few months or more, sometime less. I knew the moment the onslaught started. Before I felt any pain, a recognizable, familiar sense would slowly rise the same way as the lie I mentioned. Slow at first, like a gentle tap on the door from a long-lost friend. Then without notice the friend became the enemy and my head pounded for three days. The throbbing pain became so bad I would have a powerful urge to slam my head on the counter over and over. I knew it would not work, but aching grabbed me like a vice grip clamping down with ugly unholy pain. I feel so much compassion for people who have to endure this despicable disease.

Not sure why, but I knew the first moment, the non-benevolent migraine cracked the door. I knew it prepared to stick around tormenting for three days with horrible excruciating pain accompanying me day and night. Then, like a fever breaking, no more pain. I do not know why three days and not four or two, I only know it always remained for three days. This issue stayed with me into my late-twenties. "Here it comes, three days" became my well-practiced grinding song. Somehow, I learned how to back off, shift, and leave the pain on the door step outside my head. If I could take pride, I would sell a "How to overcome Migraines.", but I have no idea. Still don't.

This brings me to my descriptive understanding, which oddly enough contains physical attributes.

The accusing lie, "THIS IS NOT REAL. I ACTUALLY EXIST SOMEWHERE ELSE," attacks me in the same way migraines once did. Hard to explain, but the best analogy I can convey. Instead of rocketing pain in my skull, the lie slithers like a slimy snake wanting to get into my guts. When it makes the way in, I can only say it feels like I am bent over struggling for breath all the while people ask me, "How are you doing?" *Horrible, worse than horrible I want to answer,* but they do not see me with my insides turned in knots, bending over moaning wanting to scream at the top of my lungs. In my despair, I realized they only see me standing upright, with glassy eyes and maybe a slight sunken chin. I learned not blame anyone. Bless them, they have so many worries, difficulties, troubles, I could never be a real concern. It is not their fault, but this is a huge issue for me. Not a complaint or false sense of truth to believe any other organic life form might step outside themselves and truly resonate. I found a few throughout my life, who sincerely understand with their guts crimped, squeezed and tied in knots. Only a few and I am grateful. Interesting enough, most of these resonators live or lived behind the eight ball of judgment, being looked down on, whispered about by society. I learned early on I did not like being looked down on and called weird, nuts, stupid plus the big one which takes the cake, "What is wrong with you?"

I believe my father, who only thought good of me and declared excessive encouraging words of my value loud and often, helped me to stay under the radar and blind to the mocking eye of self-focused peripherally challenged society. But my father did not go with me to school, so I learned fast to cheat, fake, pivot and avoid. It did not always work. Sometimes I oozed out a bit of crazy, but recovered quickly with a joke or change of conversation. Most of my resonators learned a different path. Open, honesty and endurance under a barrage of constant powerful accusation from both pointy headed liberals (PROGRESSIVES) and square headed, (CONSERVITIVES) the same. But I digress.

Moving on.

I may get a bit rambling here as I turn down a few twisted trails into the bushes, where I still have wounded old scrapes, I should have stomped to death years ago, so I will try to remain coherent.

I will try my best.

We are all people and I have been ineffective to extinguish many of the little tiny evil familiar thoughts and flaming missiles pounding into my thoughts over and over. Most of the time I lived like an overcoming champ. I could write stories of my glory, normality and truly clear sane power, but now I have to bow down to reality. It is not anything I can be proud of, but I do not bend into shame standing outside me to drill into my soul. This is to say I have a traveling bone pulling at both sides of my sanity and I can get side tracked, over on the other side of understanding, but I feel compelled to keep going, so I will continue, with an earnest desire to spill my guts wide and far with a few questions.

Putting the lie in the rearview where it belongs, I will move to some questions I ponder which sprout weeds of my struggle. I know I have a brain. What about my mind? I have a physical beating heart, but what about my personality? Some say a soul, others a spirit, either way; I am me, alive in a body which is not me. My brain is biological tissue and with no denial, is proven to exist. Now it cannot keep going if the rest of my systems are not active. My mind on the other hand is an intangible science can study and analyzed with no certain conclusion. Assumptions yes, quasi diagnosis, sure, chemical or cognitive treatment, but somewhere on the other side of certainty. Behavior change, verbal confirmation, but false statements can create bad practices for treatment. How can you prove joy or sorrow, excitement or grief, anticipation, fear? Interpretation based on personal resonance of an emotional experience? I guess, but clearly not provable, only an unanswered mystery.

A tumor, heart disease, broken limb, fever, are treatable based on scientific fact. Your temperature is high, take this. We found a tumor; we can cut it out. You broke your arm we can fix it. No way to cut out a soul or mind, thoughts or feelings. No way to repair or bandage a broken heart. Only thing left is through chemical intervention, talking and taking notes with suggestions. Lick a finger and see which way the wind blows. Throw it against the wall and see what sticks?

Our minds and souls are unchartered territory with limited navigation. Countless thick books, endless philosophy, decades of study, but no X-ray or other diagnostic imaging exists to snap a picture of our mind, our fear, anticipation, hope, faith, terror.

We all have the same colored biological brains and pulsing hearts, but our minds and souls are unique, individual, and separate. High blood pressure and diabetes are treatable with medication. The results have actual tests to confirm effectiveness. The mind on the other hand is experimental. Try this and tell us how you feel, been feeling, and then we may or may not up or lower the dose. Or worse yet, change the chemical or add another one.

What the hell.

If you believe Jesus Christ raised Lazarus from the dead, Moses split the Red Sea, Jonah in the belly of the whale, the walls of Jericho crumpled, women coming from the rib of the FIRST man, or the big one of all, GOD SAID, "LET THERE BE LIGHT and there was light," no problem. Miracles, the unexplainable faith, are completely acceptable in most of society. No counseling needed. No drugs to see if your belief is cured. But if you sleep little because your mind is firing on extra cylinders, sparking incredible ideas, there may be an issue needing treatment. I get it. Makes sense to me. But the treatment and diagnosis are anything but clear. I feel sad, you're depressed. My thoughts race, you are manic. I believe things are not real, psychosis. Hear voices, panic, irrational fear, paranoid, the list goes on. All from checking boxes on a form and talking for a few minutes. Let's try this and see if it works? We have heard good things. Oops that did not work, try this dosage it helps people with other diseases it may be helpful. A Guiney pig, a lab rat, with only a maybe, and this is science? Mental health is a great field. Get a PHD. Send your child into shit loads of debt and years of sitting behind a desk listening, reading and sweating over the correct answers no one can even begin to prove. What a magnificent world. PSYCOLOGY! PSYCHIATRY! Mental science with organic beings who can answer questions on a test, in a dingy state funded classroom, and get a printed piece of paper called a degree are called experts. An over expensive degree with no scientific qualifications or sound philosophies other than decades of MAYBE, COULD BE, TRY THIS, MIGHT

HELP, WE SAW IT BEFORE, PUT THIS CHMEICALS DOWN YOUR THOAT, or let's talk about YOUR issues. This is the same field, great name right. FIELD. (Playing Field or maybe Practice Field) who believed in the LOBOTOMY not too many years ago.

A LOBOTOMY? Are you kidding me? Got to trust the experts.

"A lobotomy, or leucotomy, is a form of psychosurgery, a neurosurgical treatment of a mental disorder that involves severing connections in the brain›s prefrontal cortex. Most of the connections to and from the prefrontal cortex, the anterior part of the frontal lobes of the brain, are severed."

YIPPEE.

"They used this as approved treatment for psychiatric and occasionally other conditions as a mainstream procedure in some Western countries for more than two decades, despite general recognition of frequent and serious side effects. While some people experienced symptomatic improvement with the operation, they achieved the improvements at the cost of creating other impairments. The procedure was controversial from its initial use in part due to the balance between benefits and risks. Today, lobotomy has become disparaged. The procedure is a byword for medical barbarism and an exemplary instance of the medical trampling of patients' rights." Someone else wrote that. I copied and pasted here.

Let me use my words.

The big dogs, the sinister sneaky, underhanded, scum bags, with super-duper diplomas who the government gave the power to drill into your skull and insert a thin steel piece of metal into the mush of your brain and go wild, twisting left or right, up or down, deep or shallow at the will of their own fancy, while given the thumbs up to proceed even though the procedure is barbarity.

A completely disproven, grotesque, sick, heinous act, arrogant losers with big degrees used to screw every patient who bent their knee and opened their brain with hope of possible deliverance and in the end, became ZOMBIES. This sick, obviously worthless, and destructive procedure by the highly educated quacks who's offspring peddle meds for billion-dollar "BIG PHARMA." They called them BIG PHARMA now. Isn't that awesome? Or horrible? What a name and clear description as they remain invisible and undercover. But they make sure their half-baked chemical treatment become the mainstream. Brilliant, outstanding. Investing in their stocks might be the best option. Go crazy, get addicted, but get a huge return?

A neurosurgical treatment which drilled into brains like an amateur auto mechanic trying to unclog a stopped-up pipe while they mashed the mush together. How in the world, and this became a sanctioned procedure? Stick a bar into a brain and move it around in a sweet rotation. I still believe most logical thinking human beings might come to a consensus. Who knows the world seems to tilt off the axis of common sense these days? I could be wrong, but who cares. Their barbarism only increased experientially. Stop treatment by drilling into the brain or attached some electrodes to the skull and send electricity pulsating across the fleshy tissue containing the mind. I believe they call it "SHOCK THERAPY" and they still provide this option at your friendly neighborhood head shrinker. Maybe they should just go all the way and cut your head off, mount it on the wall and ask the question. "How do you feel now?" Tell me the difference? Oh wait, a detached head from the body makes the lab rat no longer available to say if the treatment worked. Plus, they would no longer be around so health insurance companies can reimburse for the cesspool of mind-altering drugs.

A real bummer.

Give a pill to shallow and have them come back. Go out into the big bad world, interact, go nuts, get arrested, then come back and we will ask a few unsympathetic questions and try again. Over and over, but with the sheer clear purpose to get a study so the Psychotherapist might get a few PATS ON THE SHOULDER and FASLE ADMIRATION. Studies, big studies, to say, this did good for this crazy one and that really held some value for that one. But when some of the lab rats kill themselves, it seems as if no one but those who loved the struggling souls really cared. Where are the studies on the lack of success? The failures and absolute truth, this is not science, assumption based, best guest with massive failure.

Am I preaching to a soundless hurricane?

Why would a third-party payor approve such snake oil procedures? Because BIG INSURANCE became duped and they cower to slimy LAW MAKERS all the while they raise insurance premiums to cover the costs and keep profitable.

Mental health treatment is like trying to predict when and where an earthquake, tornado or hurricane will cause destruction. It does not rain all year. Is treatment of the mind seasonal?

Just a question.

I said I could get a bit rambling, but I believe I will circle around and keep flowing down the rushing river of the rapids I surfed all my life without too many detours.

I decided a year and a half ago to stop thinking up and acting on ideas swirling across the manic imagination I spent my whole life living under as a tranquilizer to keep me from coming apart at the seams. I took a sovereign vow for my health, to not start a new business, buy another house or property and finally deal with my escaping, hidden, covering up ways. A huge issue for me and it did not come naturally. I fought internally like a disobedient rebellious adolescent with wailing fists against a powerful familiar authority inside myself. No other person heard or knew my difficultly and painful frustration rushing with overpowering torrents in my soul. I stood alone against the onslaught, my bare toes digging as deep as possible hoping to keep from being bulldozed and swept down a dark cold endless stream into nothingness. I worked to stand like an unmovable stone, bent down and accepted a self-inflicted prohibition against hiring people to carry out my whack-a-doddle, cockamamie ideas, no matter how fantastic they might be. I shut down cold turkey. No more, never again, and I held firm with faithful obedience.

For decades I spent most of my waking hours and countless nights dreaming up the ridiculous and putting my whole effort into seeing the imaginary visions materialize in this physical world. Thank God he did not let me go bankrupt, burn in failure, and left destitute in a bottomless ditch. A couple ideas produced fruit and revenue; the others crashed and burned in a pile of smoldering ash. Failure did not concern me, I only thought, *don't matter, I have this NEW, brand new idea, and it is beyond awesome.* This became a potent medication to keep me from looking inward, digging deep, pulling back the dark curtain I lived with since my first recollection. Looking back, I am amazed no one called me out, but I realized a long time ago, people focus on their own issues so they live blind beyond actual perception so I used the perfect excuse to hide in open site beyond my disguise as an engaged father and ridiculous business man. It worked like a charm for nearly three decades, with only a few dozen stumbles. No one really noticed as the cracks shined the light of truth at my darkness.

What a wonderful world.

When you keep busy, serve, sacrifice, say yes to every request, and act in charge while bringing in more bacon than you deserve, no questions are asked. Then I got side swiped. The Beautiful Perfect Seven grew up; I sold properties by the skin of my teeth and sold the lion share of my businesses. In the end, I found myself in a different world. A brand-new world. One I never experienced before. With a stream of revenue flowing in without much need to work, I made a conscious choice to stop saying yes, stop dabbling with new ideas, I literally slapped my hand when my mind saw the light of a new invention or business. The hand I slapped over and over became red and puffy, with clearly outlined welts, by no one noticed. Then I bowed my life down, crumbled and cave to nothingness. I took the risk to find myself with myself. I must say I came up with some of the most incredible ideas during this time, but I worked my heart out to press down, crush, stomp to death and silence those old ways of thinking. Might seem easy, but for me it felt like tons of iron, and piles of rock unloaded on me to make me give in or die. I never did well at lifting weights. Pull ups, push-ups were no problem, but pressing iron never fit my demeanor. In this season, I gritted my teeth in agony to lift all the heavy weights and rocks off my soul. Not a simple task. I knew I held in my back pocket the option to go back to my old ways and deny, avoid, fake, smile and say yes to any request, but I chose to lift and push, turn and grit my way through.

I made a commitment to stop cold turkey and in faithfulness, then all hell unleashed on me. Horrifying, disgusting emotions, regrets, uncontrollable crying and moaning ensued and I felt an overwhelming temptation to get busy, but I didn't. I floated in my pool and spend time realizing how ridiculous many of the decisions I made were. Utterly ridiculous. I spent most of my adult life rolling the dice over and over, time and again, putting every idea I dreamed up on the table all in. A healthcare administration firm, prescription drug card, Low powered television station, online drop shipping stores, software company, ultra-low film production company, and health insurance brokerage, just to name a few. Most utterly failed, but a couple still bring in revenue without too much work, so I had plenty of time to dig down internally and reflect. It did not turn out good. The weirdest part became the wide flowing tears. Uncontrollable convulsing, moaning, crying at any moment out of the blue. In a supermarket, gas station, watching a movie. Just weird for no apparent reason, not sadness or grief or shame. I had regrets, but they did not cause the flowing tears. The weeping came and went for no seemingly good reason. I burst out, turned my face away and within ten to twenty seconds all gone.

Depression seemed to be the undeniable obvious diagnosis. I could agree except I went through a crippling, grotesque depression at the age of twenty-one. The worst, no question, hands down. Horrible. I slept sixteen hours a day for months. My guts became turned inside out and twisted in crushing, gripping knots. These outbursts of tears were not that type of depression, maybe a unique form. A better form, but I really did not feel depressed. Just flowing tears from nowhere. So much better, trust me. Sleeping most of the day and night is the absolute worst. Pouring out salty tears for no known reason is nothing, although clearly an anomaly. A strange anomaly, I agree, but better than crippling wrenching gut strangling depression. I sat up and stood in a bit of sanity. Clearly, I did not have the horrible depression from decades back. Those who loved me could not hear, although I tried to explain.

I went to several healthcare professionals who ordered brain imaging and the full gambit of heart, blood and every other test under the sun. Other than being low in vitamin D, all came back clear. The highly educated professionals prescribed a slight anti-depressant, which I did not take. I cheated instead. I still put aside thoughts of new brilliant business ideas and did not say yes to every request coming my way. I looked this abnormal transition in the eye and did not back down. Why shallow medication to not feel an abnormality. Embrace the change, get to the bottom of the actual causes. This did not cripple my life, it only sent odd emotions flipping somersaults around my heart. The end product surely created questions, most if not all would question, but I decided to go full-bore, head to head, to see without denial. To say I battled internally would be a drastic understatement, but I was not laying in a bed crippled, unable to function so this felt like a hitting the lottery.

During this time, I believed I contained what I would say is a sound minded clarity. Looking back, I may agree I should have asked for help, but let's be clear, no going back. None of us can. Unless I am wrong, please tell me how.

The biggest, most poignant issue, the one pointing an undeniable finger of accusation of abnormality, is the outburst of tears, no question. People do not start crying for no given reason on the spot, out in the open, out of the blue. I get it, I got it than. I knew these tears were not from grief, sorrow over my actions and deeds. They came like the flapping wings of birds taking flight at a moment's notice without reason. I know I had regrets about my personal life, thoughts and actions over decades, but these tears came from another source, a source I could not put a finger on, then I felt slapped across the face and spanked by the principle of the universe. Rebuked with a hot bright light against my nature. An undeniable shining light bringing down the gavel of guilt against how I lived, how I existed, covered up, cheated and avoided.

With nothing to do and a full-time ability to reflect, my ridiculous life unfolded before me and I saw without excuse all the times I protected myself from coming to grips with who I am through abdication, avoidance and downright cheating. Not good. Not good at all, but hey, I found this out in silence, internally. I held compassion, real and true concern for others, for sure and stepped out on countless occasions, acted, behind the scenes to give, help, or whatever, from a true heart hidden in a genuine desire, no question, at least I thought. I can look back and I know my heart wanted to give, but I now understand I acted blind with pride-based ignorance. Shame on me. At the time, I did not know. This is not an excuse, only a confession of self-focused protective ignorance which brought a bright shining rebuke of the most uncomfortable illumination. I gave, served, showed compassion from a place of prosperity and pride.

My dichotomy is truly wanting to give or help, only to find out the origins came from seeds planted in selfishness and reaped in arrogance, did not fill me with cuddly warmth. As I pondered my wheelie ways, the tears flowed thicker and came faster from thoughts of others, not from my own short comings. I did not grieve specific actions, times or places. I understood they were out of self-protection; I could not go back and change anything. I stood accused and guilty. The issue became my motive not my actions. My heart and mind. The true reason behind how and why I did all I did unfolded, so I stopped giving and stopped trying to help. My childish answer seemed to be a solution to overcome my tweaked new existence. In my mind I thought the issue of my difficultly resided in my view point. How I observed the outside world, those around me and my ignorant philosophies rooted in my deceived perception of my superiority.

I believe there is a value in coming to grips with short comings. Looking deeply into the often-hidden motives behind actions seems to be a perfect place for introspection. Action and decisions flowing from a true pure stream produce fruit in unseen realms with long-lasting gratification. Those good works or deeds from a polluted place need to be uprooted and burned. My answer became a prohibition on giving or helping others until and only until, I knew my motivation came from an un-contaminated source. It did not happen. A real bummer. I assumed my new found revelation would produce a breakthrough. Instead I found myself spinning in the wind looking for an anchor to tether to and found myself with no counter measure.

My vow did not work.

Then I came up with another brilliant valueless idea. Walk in blindness. As I mentioned, in the sixth grade I experienced the worst type of migraine headaches and they came back with an inhumane vengeance out of the blue for no real discernible reason over and over. Migraines? What a name. Sounds scientific or some obscure definition in old English or Latin to keep those who suffer stymied? A cool name, but inadequate to describe throbbing pain through your entire head and all quadrants dripping through your body, not with pain, instead by way of nauseating fatigue producing frustration and fierce anger.

Wearing corrective lenses became a side product which has been part of my life ever since. For a time, I only needed them to read and drive as the heart pounding headaches continued for years until they subsided, but my eyesight steadily needed deeper correction. So much so, I could not read a digital clock two feet away without my glasses. Through delusion, ignorance, or embryonic hope, I decided to take my glasses off whenever I found myself around strangers. Grocery stores, banks, gas stations, post office, everywhere. If I could not see faces, I found myself less emotionally volatile. The spontaneous tears stopped in public. No glasses and I could not see faces, or life's difficulty in their expressions. Blurry site worked like a charm. I could only see a few feet in front of me without spectacles, but it became enough to alter the strange emotional outburst in public.

My eyes were not the issue, but keeping them from clear sight helped more than I could say.

I literally believed my difficulty came from all I saw if my sight was twenty / twenty. Half blind, I struggled to read labels or prices without putting them two inches from my face, but a beneficial trade off.

Although much of my emotional upheaval subsided in public, it continued in private and opened up a deep time of reflection and contemplation. I took time to investigate the actions and decisions over my life and came to a place of understanding and disappointment.

Regrets flooded my heart as I went from a thousand miles an hour to zero, with a commitment internally to not race around and do something else, regrets came sweeping in with an unbenevolent vengeance. I opened up and allowed my overall nature to unfold. I put away, with a powerful effort, the way I acted my entire life. In return an awesome and terrifying revelation took hold. I found myself unprepared without training, no grid to maneuverer, shift and cover up, but I pressed forward. Looking back, I would say, "DO NOT DO IT," but here I am now and exposed. Naked on the side of an icy rocky incline going straight up into utter darkness. Unchartered territory. A no-man's-land containing claustrophobic isolation with a chilling albatross around my neck. Four big fat oozing regrets. No specifics, as I only lived high above the clouds, in my own twisted mind. I think this is where the gushes of tears come from. The individual regrets bigger than I can engage in are a huge issue, but I will leave the particulars on the doorstep for another day.

A day I hope never arrives.

The regrets pointing true accusation against me came from a broad and wide spectrum, not individual and not detailed. A long overview, not one person, conversation, day or time. Four big-picture regrets not the thousands of painful micro ones. I am not there yet. Too much for my broken mind to endure for a while maybe ever, so I will press on to highlight the essence of these regrets the Seven lived under to my never-ending shame.

Opinions

Not a big word, seems kind of small. An Opinion. My opinions. What I think. My philosophy. But if you use it as a weapon, then damage takes place no mechanic can diagnosis. WOUNDS. PAIN. Lifelong difficulty ensues and I am the inflictor. I used the sharp loaded weapon of my opinion nearly my whole life and I had a powerful persuasive ability. I will not go through all the times I spouted, preached, poured out my opinion into the hearts and minds of the Seven. If I could suck back those arrogant, persuasive words and selfish philosophical ideas I would, before you can say, "Jack is your Uncle," but no way to go back. I will not go into the specifics of the uncountable times I interrupted, gave my pre-determined truth and unfeeling diatribes in response to mothers, fathers, business people, employees and on and on, but the worst is the times I interrupted, and spouted my opinions to my seven children. My tweaked, self-focused philosophies guided my words, and they sounded great, better than great, biblical in fact and I am ashamed. If heaven could hold up a mirror and play back, I would stand accused, wrong and guilty. I knowingly spoke with selfish and unreasonable interruption, and took over when the beautiful perfect seven opened up their hearts, fears, hopes and desires. I can never go back, but if I had such a magical clock to turn back the clock, I would listen, bite my tongue, and allow all seven to speak while I listened and put my arms around them, but fantasy does not have real value so I accept my sinful and blind ways. I am working to not give any opinions. I am working to LISTEN AND HEAR. Not an effortless task as I spent most of my adult life stating every cockamamie opinion my mind conjured as poisonous fruit from the seed of my second regret.

Pride

An ugly part of myself came into view while I shut off my old ways of dreaming up new and awesome ideas giving way to another crystal-clear regret. Arrogance, hubris, ugly pride. I existed under a dark shadow for most of my existence battling against being called stupid, weird, one with problems, a looked down upon little abnormal creature. The one who would not succeed. I did not realize the impact these negative curses had over me. I bypassed the accusations with unhealthy counter-measures. I rejected each curse with a spirit of pity toward those who cast them upon me. I stood firm with an arrogant heart. A haughty demeanor, shifting gears to look down on so many. This came about not through anger or bitterness but a false sense of superiority I held deep inside.

What is pride? I am proud of the Seven. They are absolutely outstanding, incredible. The greatest out of billions across the planet hands down, no question. Being proud of my children is not the pride I am talking about. Thinking I am better than others is the worst kind of pride. Believing my intellect, achievements, talents, gifts, successes, made me better, more important, more deserving than others and not just a few. Many. Most others. I spent decades watering, tending and protecting my hubris, until I received a massive rebuke against my own corrupt nature. An opposing force stood against me. The maker of the never-ending universe opposes the proud but gives grace to the humble. I lived with a false sense of humility and oozed porous deceitful pride. Opposition can come from many places at any time big or small. The absolute strongest is unquestionably GOD.

When I slowed down long enough, I came face to face with the shadowy deception I planted in my mind and saw with an unfiltered illumination how truly disgusting my pride is. No hole seemed big enough to bury my head, so I held firm and took time to address my inexcusable obnoxious pride. I sensed the smell of the toxic stench then I understood the origins. The bastard child called Judgment.

Judgment

The seeds producing thoughts of my false sense of superiority, came from deep rooted unjustified instant judgement towards others around me without discrimination. I judged everyone with no partiality. I lived under a shadow of preconceived, intolerable verdicts against nearly every other creature I came into contact with for an unknown reason, but it does not matter. I am guilty without excuse. Internally I made some type of vow to never spin back into the darkest place I escaped in my early twenties. The crippling, evil depression. I created an unsophisticated but powerful protective mechanism, or an elaborate self-protective denial system, I do not know. I did not pounder thoughts of suicide. Instead, I went in the other direction with an unexplainable deception. I programmed myself to evaluate in a moment and passed judgement on others. I allowed my mind to fill up with massive pious opinions, countless areas of arrogant pride based on a deceptive comfort in judging others.

Three twisted interlocked gnarled deadly branches. Opinions from pride based in judgment. A painful reality I allowed myself to bent under while I lived to keep myself from feeling or experiencing the bitter truth. A major part of who I am, who I always have been, is out of balance and needs attention. The problem is at my core. It could be a physical imbalance in my brain or a tweaked out of order psychological issue in my mind. Either way, I came to a place of no return. I decided never to go back to my old ways of mentally running away through ideas, opinions, pride and judgment. I looked my regrets straight in the eye and did not like the evil staring back. I saw myself, my nature but could not snap my fingers and never again speak my opinion or feel pride or judge. It is very difficult to unravel a cord of three interwoven unhealthily attitudes used as protection to not go into the crippling black hole of hopeless depression.

Interesting enough I have spoken some of these thoughts to people who seem to struggle over the word regret more than the substance of my pride filled judgements or self-deluded worthless opinions. It may be all of society or the community I live in changed, but somehow the word regret does not go over well. Another one is shame. It seems as if a shift took place I did not notice. The new do's and don'ts come in weird stripes. "Don't have regrets, don't feel shame, don't deny yourself, do put up boundaries, do love yourself, do find your happiness. It used to be don't commit adultery, kill or steal and do love your neighbor. So, regret, shame and denial are taboo.

Who knew?

Instead of regret let me use unfamiliar words. I realized, recognized, acknowledged, understood, identified, the uncomfortable and undeniable reality I hid under for years behind a cement curtain. To keep me from spinning out of control, I verbally afflicted others, overlooked others, looked down on others, interrupted others, spouted endless diatribes, mocked, shook my head in disgust, and in general, lived as a selfish worthless piece of shit. I guess I loved myself, I put up boundaries, worked to be happy. It did not work and I feel massive regret and utter shame.

It takes a balancing act to untie three sinister parts of yourself. The three cords wrapped so tightly they overlap at a moment's notice. See a person and "click," judgment, "click" pride and the big "click," opinion. One, two, three, quicker than a snap of the fingers. Lickety-split.

As an example:

A man, does not matter the color, age or clothing, holds a bent piece of cardboard. "Will work for food."

A woman in a grocery store yelling at her children.

A sales person boasting about a big deal they closed.

A parent declares their children and will go to the ivy league, but they have to work very hard.

A preacher who talks of the clear spirit of grace leavened with heaping shovels of rules.

A school teacher more interested in the teacher's union than the students.

An atheist who shows more compassion for the poor than the religious pious talkers.

A pot smoking teenager with more wisdom than an eighty-year-old.

These are a few as an illustration where I would spin and turn on the preverbal mental dime. Judgment first, pride second, opinion third. Looking back, I came to see; I am the worst of the worst. Running through the streets with sack cloth and ashes, screaming my head off, is not the answer, but I seriously considered the act. I contemplated the scene. Imagine the tons of thumbs up and followers on social media, but pride abides in acknowledgment of strangers. It also can produce revenue, I get it, but let's not go down that path.

I understood I only held a slight amount of control over one of three. Thoughts of judgement and pride came at lightning speed. I became well practiced at receiving the signal of accusation, attributing reasons based on unfounded preconceptions, sealing my judgment in granite.

Nothing I could do about the thoughts. They came like a flood from all directions and flowed in before I could I could raise up a shield or erect a dam to stop them. Right or wrong, accurate or complete sinister lies, bombarded my thoughts faster they I knew or could do anything to combat or stop the influx. Thoughts come and go leaving a lingering fading trail, but never fully erase from memory and feeling.

A clear revelation occurred to me. Pride and judgment were not the place I could affect change. Only my tongue held power. Not giving, stating my opinion, not speaking at all, keeping my mouth shut, became the powerful one of three I held authority over.

To say this new found understanding held power to bring a change to set me free and set me on a path to normality, might be the smallest, embryonic thought I ever allowed to seep into my mind. But it held extreme power. If I kept my mouth shut, then most if not all would never materialize. An intense battle ensued. The more I tried to hold my tongue, not give an opinion, listen to others, the more I moved up and down internally in dramatic spikes with some strange outward manifestations. I felt as if I belted myself into an emotional rollercoaster I could not get off.

The flowing tears bursting out in public did not last long each time but not a good issue. On the other side of the coin I would find myself in a simple conversation with a clerk at a store, or a vendor, usually on the phone, and an irrational irritation or frustration would bubble at first and then bellow in my guts over nothing. Simple words. "It will be ten cents a bag sir." This became a law in the state I live in so people pay twenty bucks for reusable bags they carry into the store to save the ten cents per. I would say, "No problem," on the outside, but inside I would think, how can we as human beings shift our behavior so easily. Ten cents a bag? Wow. Then my thought would zing to "I know it is an additional fee per bag, you told me this for a year. Will there be a time when I will not need to be told? Apparently not for the airlines. In case you're not aware, no smoking on planes, even in the lavatories. Tell everyone the same declaration on every flight for decades.

I understand, this seems small, I do. But it did not keep me from going from a simmer to a boil. Mostly I controlled myself, gave a half-baked smile all the while I felt like bright white steam whistled from my ears. And don't get me started on the thirty percent discounts if you use this card, or you get these discounts by putting your phone number in, the unlimited gigs for only twenty bucks more. The per line must be in the unspoken small print. I could go on and on and on, but why belabor the point. I stared to come apart at the seams. Crying for no reason on one hand, wanting to scream my head off on the other, while I fought to not give my opinion, or roll the financial dice on the few crazy business ideas rattling like tempting intruders in my mind. Instead of saying what I thought or acting on a vision, tears and irritation came. Not a fair exchange, but I committed myself to hold firm and not go back to wild risk-taking living.

I spent years, decades making hundreds of decisions a day, family, business, friends, buying things, working with vendors, selling, creating, paying employees, on an on. No problem. I juggled, served, dictated, decided all without thought or consideration riding high, flowing well. I lived in the macro, but could engage in the micro when needed but for only a few moments.

Then I went all stop and reflected on my life. I spent an exhausting six months contemplating, evaluating, recognizing many aspects of how I lived which brought me to the brink of insanity so I found a vice, actually three.

The wonder of the Beautiful Perfect Seven, information and fantasy.

Thoughts of the perfect seven kept my mind from coming all the way apart. One problem, they became the receivers of my half-baked opinions over the years, a fact I will always regret, so a double whammy lingered on the recesses of my thoughts. All in all, the tremendous power of their existence won the battle over my short comings. I shifted and worked to listen to hear the seven. I tried not to talk, and understand, but in the end my choice changed the dynamic and not all for the good. Four were adults, on their own, so I chose to accept any decision they made and think the best of them. No advice, unless they asked specifically. No opinion period. I would even say the phrase, "I am sorry I do not have an opinion, but I know you have wisdom." The awesome power of the seven became an anchor to keep me from completely spinning out, but I still flapped around battered by the winds of emotional upheaval so I medicated myself without knowing. We live in an informational age where your thumb can swipe across a small glass screen and the whole wide world is at your fingertips and I let my finger do the walking to the max.

The orange man became president and an endless plethora of political battles waged back and forth on a daily basis, almost hourly. Fantastic for someone who needed a distraction, and I took full advantage, hook line and sinker. I became a fiend. BBC, Fox News, MSNBC, CNN, ABC, NPR. I woke in the dark, made coffee and let my fingers slip and slide. It would be obsessive to say I read or listened to everything, I didn't. Only seventy percent on all platforms, no exaggeration. I had all the apps set to politics so there were other things happening around the world I did not look at.

I listened, read, studied, all sides daily, actually most of the day. Wall to wall and bumper to bumper. Impeachment, wall to wall. Special counsel report bumper to bumper. Then I would read and listen to the talking heads on both sides and laugh out loud. Because I got rid of opinion, I relished listening to others who seemed to get tied into intellectual knots giving all matter of opinions and the orange man sparked the fire for all of them. An incredible frenzy ensued and became a fantastic medicine for me. Love or hate the orange man you who have to admit, a shaking occurred. I understand the severity of decisions, the true-life impact of the political battle on people and society, but I do not have control, I am not the one in authority, so I watched, and listened and laughed. The tears subsided, the irritation simmered down, the regrets seemed to move to the back seat and I went into a place of quasi normality. A hibernation with the help of another medicine. Fantasy as an art and craft. I wrote a long form novel with many characters, wild worlds, life, death, pain, sorrow and grief along with a healthy dose of hope and possibility. Then a crack broke in the dam of my new found stability. Obsession. I came to realize I held in me an unbalanced ability to get obsessed.

This is not good. Not good at all.

Interesting enough I did not see my addiction to political theater as an obsession, although it clearly was. Wake up boy. The story I created, the characters, their struggles, where they would go, what they would do, consumed me. It started with a simple idea. Two identical twin brothers, one weak and one strong, in this world, but when they find themselves in another world, the tide flips and the powerful brother is the weak one. Simple idea. Before I knew it, the two brothers had twelve other characters in their story and I had hundreds of pages of made up people, who I absolutely loved, with no idea where they would end up. I didn't care. The thrill I received from the process became a sweet tonic, until, obsession. I could not keep my mind off the story. Where they would go, what would happen. It felt like watching a great movie on the edge of your seat over months. Awesome, except when it becomes an obsession.

In conversations with people, I would nod and mumble, all the while I contemplated how one of my beloved characters might go through the fire or die. Oh no! When it started happening with the seven, I stopped writing the story and forced my mind to not think about it. It became less difficult than I thought. Once out of sight, it went out of my mind. It is okay because the orange man started making bigger waves. Yahoo. I still had my phone as a sweet little Binky.

For months I did not write a single word in the book, nor did I let my imagination drift or wonder. Well it wondered all over the place, but not to the world and people I made up. After a season, several months I came back to the project with a simple thought. Take a character from one place to another and then stop writing and do not think about it until the next time. This worked well, great in fact. I started writing each day sometimes for an hour sometimes longer, but when I got from one place to the next, I stopped. This took away the obsession to think about made up people and places when in conversation with others.

I did not understand at the time, but came to see, I spent most of my life holding several conversations or thoughts in my mind at the same time. As I went back to work on my story, scene to scene, or place to place, I had the book on one side of my sleek, thin wide screen monitor, hooked to my computer, and several tabs to online news channels on the other plus a streaming movie. I would click back and forth with the talking heads and then pushed play on the movie while I wrote the novel. Never did I write without people talking or acting. I literally wrote many scenes which turned into pretty long and well formatted chapters while the bumper to bumper impeachment hearings went on. I wrote while movies or documentaries played. I never wrote in silence. I understand this is outside of normal, but I did not care. The tears left, wild thoughts were taking a respite, irritation simmered down, I lived opinion free and I finished the first draft of a pretty fat novel.

Looking back, I understand political news stimulated my mind to keep at bay my true nature. Writing a wide-reaching story became medicine to my soul until I finished it. I have a number of other stories I could have delved right into, but I found myself feeling sick, literally at the thought. Something left me empty after completing a significant work of fiction. I am not sure how to explain the feeling, only to say the effort took something out of me. It is okay, because I wasn't looking to get rich or famous, I loved the process. I printed out one copy, two sided, held it in my hands and thought I never want to do one like this again. Six months later, I broke apart.

The break

An abundance of outstanding information can keep the mind lubricated. Watching and reading the back-and-forth bantering from unbelieving talking heads with red faces kept me from tipping out of stability. Some thinking they might have caught the scoundrel with grizzled meat clamped in their teeth, others defending the orange man turning them themselves into illogical knots became a real treat to watch. The talkers all made millions of dollars with enormous staffs of people getting graphics lined up for the next addition but they were spitting into the wind. The whole thing made me laugh and as I said, the tears went away, turned off and evaporated. Perfect medication. So amazing. The advertisers made a bundle. The peddlers who need eye balls to pitch thirty seconds on high definition to hook the masses came out like bandits. What a great country. With a few swipes of my thumbs on my pocket scene I went from tears to mocking laughter. Technology is incredible. The daily rollercoaster of the "news casters" worked. At least for a time.

The right, the left, progressives and conservatives twisting and turning in the wind. The small-minded spastic orange man lived for decades as a liberal narcissist than he jumped three degrees past the sincerest conservative only to turn numerous ivy league hypocrite elites on their pointy heads barking and squawking with puffy frustrated faces. Such excellent medicine. Then social distancing and social unrest appeared back to back, and I found myself rebuked. The world changed, and I got caught as a cynical hypocrite and broke into pieces. My medicine or drug or escape into an abnormal amount of political information stabbed me in the heart and snapped my mind wide open.

I spent five decades, and I never heard the phrase SOCIAL DISTANCING. Six feet is the distance. Might be two arm lengths as an answer, but who knows. Science and data became the words of war. Science and data. I thought sure, shut down, nobody knows and how horrible. Take every precaution necessary. I am in, all in, until the facts, science and data seeped out. The undeniable truth shined bright with undeniable clarity. The new variety of flu strain spread like a sinister silent killer across the planet with unconscionable speed. The target of the bullseye landed on the weak, disabled, sick and the elderly who inadvertently found themselves in the crosshairs of the disgusting virus. The crown virus as if it held a regal attribute could kill those at risk. The vulnerable. The universal order to stay at home, social distance and open your phones for contact tracking came like a flood as the answer. Okay this is different. The poor, sick, and the elderly stand like bowling pins at risk. The mass majority of those infected never knew it infected them. A-typical is the word. I believe it means NEVER KNEW THEY WERE SICK. I understand they could infect the vulnerable, and we as a caring society, should have made the declaration, THE OLD, SICK, those with immune systems problems, the obese, diabetics, heart problems need to stay home. Pay them to stay home. We all would have delivered food, medicine, water and kept back thirty feet not only six to serve those at risk and in need. The entire country would get on board. No need for essential workers. No need for shut downs. As a country we could have, should have protected the vulnerable, those at risk, instead, they sent the infected into nursing care facilities and thousands died while gasping for breath. That is when information shot an arrow into my mental stability but I continued to partake. The politics I laughed at started to make me cry. Then I watched George Floyd die. Over and over and over.

Two employees of city government kneeled on his back a third on his neck and a fourth stood and watched. They killed him on camera and then SOCIAL UNREST took place. All over the place. My first thought is the advertisers, the product pushers, set this in motion. They paid to pitch so we would covet. What do they expect? They put the goods behind enormous glass windows and shine lights to enhance the desire. Why not smash the window and grab? Only my first thought, the second one trapped me. Who will be the first talking head to say the looters should social distance while they participate in social unrest? Sure, enough one did, and I began to spin out in some abnormal delusion. My mind began to unravel and my grip on reality started to slip through my fingers. The lie came to get me with a powerful side swipe and gut punch and sent me down a rabbit hole toward insanity.

During this period, I had conversations I am not sure were real or imagined. The people were real, but what I thought I said, or might have said, eluded me. I also had thoughts I do not remember, but still feel rattling through my body, or mind or emotions, not sure which. I felt as if I was living in a dream and I had difficulty knowing if I was a sleep or awake. I know I slept very little for a number of days. I did not count the hours or use a calendar. I remember having debates with myself, but unsure which side I believed. Both I guess. I had a similar experience like this other times years ago, but it only lasted a few days. Once for an entire week. Those times felt like a soft pillow compared to this iron clad wrecking ball against my psyche.

When you debate yourself on an issue you cannot recall, but still feel the emotion you know things have gone off the rail. The tears were back and this time they did not come and go, they lingered, poured out, gushed out, flooded out. I worked to hold them back and did okay, I think. My memory during this period, is worse than sinking sand, but I know I did not wail and moan and cry nonstop, that came later. I held enough sanity to know I was losing my marbles, teetering on the edge ready to go off the deep end and I feared winding up in a dark lifeless pit without a latter and no way back. Falling, falling, falling. "Help I've fallen and I can't get up."

I should have asked for help but I ran away instead.

Ten miles away from my home I found a hotel. I made it to the counter without too many ticks or twitches and no major outburst, but the attendant raised an eyebrow. I did not care. I gave her a card she swiped, and I got a card to open a door in return. I made it. Almost. I held the room key in a vice grip, but I could not find my room for the life of me. I walked in horrible anxious driven circles finding myself back where I started. I did not want to go to the front desk as I believed I might go bat shit crazy. I kept myself from yelling at the top of my lungs and moved with a determined step to find my room, but I literally felt like I entered an alternative realm where life existed on a prolonged acid trip. No hallucinations, only strange ultra-slow movement in the physical, but the map to my room seemed to be alive. Very creepy. Downright horrifying. Then a couple of angels appeared in front of me and asked if they could help. Middle aged, probably husband and wife. I cannot remember their faces, their clothes anything except their help. "Yes, Yes, Yes," I wanted to scream, "I need help," but nothing came out. I knew I was shaking like a jittering palsy inflicted whacko. "I can't find my room," I squeaked out, and they helped me.

Thank God.

The door locked behind me with an undeniable metal thud. Safe and sound. I brought nothing with me. No bags, no luggage only a thin wallet with debit and credit cards, shorts, T-shirt and sneakers, car keys and a cell phone, which I let the battery die hours before. I tossed my glasses off and dove onto the bed face down with my head in the center of a pillow and screamed out a mournful continual round of tears. I wailed loud and long. Due to the state wide shut down from COVID-19, most of the hotel remained empty, so my outbursts went unheeded, at least no one knocked on the door or walls telling me to shut up.

I arrived behind the locked hotel room on a Tuesday, early afternoon. The previous two weeks held many holes with blank spaces. Many conversations, some I remember parts of, others I struggle to recall, a miss mash of disjointed memory. The weeks long fog remains faded and I am still unable to bring to recollection, but that is not as bad as my time in the hotel room which holds almost a complete black out in memory. At least one entire day I have no recall. I lost an entire day. Eight weeks removed from that time; I have been able to piece together some disconnected parts. There are enormous gaps, filled with dark blanks, including at least fifteen hours of a total lost to memory, but the small parts I have been able to piece back together, are not flattering.

I remember at some point stumbling bare foot, but with my shorts and shirt on, to a vending machine where I used a shaky hand to swipe a credit card to buy chips, nuts, bottles of water and a sprite. I ate and drank like a bird between bouts of sobbing, talking out loud and stuttering weird rambling incoherent murmurs. Not words only gibberish over and over. I even had this outburst when I went to the vending machine. I heard a noise, as if someone might be coming toward me. Panicked I put my hand over my mouth to stop and pounded my feet on the ground to find some sort of control. No use and no one arrived. The best way to convey the sounds uncontrollably coming out of me is to type the sounds I remember. Te, te, te, te te te, la la la la la la la la. Va va va va va va va. It did not come with tears, but jerking shakes in my body. Very unsettling. This stuttering gibberish, whatever it is, would rise and fall in tone and volume and go on for extended periods and then stop out of the blue. I felt exhausted and would throw myself on the bed and cry, then go silent. The oddity of this experience made me concerned but all the other issues seemed pare for the course.

A clearly unstable course.

I know I must have slept, but I cannot for the life of me remember. I remember I had the thick dark curtains drawn and melted day to night.

I paced the room at times shaking and trembling, twitching and jerking mumbling and arguing with words I cannot remember but still feel the torment from. I stood in the corner of the room stark naked, quiet and still as a monk with blank empty thoughts, then murmuring gibberish, rolled out. For extended periods I stood, unmoving, an empty vessel naked, slumped in the shoulders, chin to my chest like a flimsy statue, then the tears came again. At times I would fall in a heap on the bed and cry uncontrollably. I know I must have nodded off a number of times, I just cannot remember how long. An hour here and an hour there is my best guess. I watched as the morning light started to crack through the window shades on what I believed to be Thursday morning. I arrived Tuesday and here came Thursday. Most nights for the last year I would be up well before dawn, watching as the sunrise started. My cell phone battery went dead days before, but I knew this time of year it must be going on six o'clock or so. I also knew I needed to snap out of this before Friday. At noon on Friday the second of the seven, was getting married. A huge deal. An enormous deal and no way I could show up in a state of crazy blabbering and moaning, shaking and twitching. I held enough sanity to know this wonderful celebration, this significant event, did not need a tweaked whacko making a scene.

As the light punched brighter cracks through the thick curtains, I focused on getting myself together. I needed to snap out of this horrifying state and get back to a place of normality. Not an effortless task.

All seven would be together for the first time in a couple of years. I needed to get a grip. My thought went to time. Thursday morning until Friday morning, at least twenty-four hours, should be a sufficient amount of time. At least I thought.

The only problem, the morning light outside, announcing a new day, turned out to be Friday and not Thursday. I found this out later and almost too late.

I used breathing exercises, deep intake slow release over and over as my weapon. I paced across the room like a stoic diligent sentry, stationed to guard against an unknown enemy. In my case I knew the enemy, dabbled with the enemy, felt as if I caved in to the enemy and may have surrendered with no hope of release. Forever altered, damaged with no way back, no hope, my lot in life forever under the unbenevolent thumb of my enemy, INSANITY.

"NO MORE," I told myself internally and verbally. "NO MORE, NO MORE!"

I did not scream and mostly not at a fevered pitch. Anger proved to not be a friend. Hostility seemed to be counterproductive. Like adding fuel to the fire. So, in an orderly, structural fashion I took deep breaths, very deep, pacing back and forth across the carpet, from door to window and back again, and again, and again, I spoke out a constant "No more," declaration over and over. At first it began to help bring me to a semi place of normality. Then the murmuring gibberish, tears and moaning rose up and out between "NO MORE, NO MORE, NO MORE." This battle went on for at least two hours. Back and forth, back and forth, while pacing back and forth.

The gift of hunger stepped in as a welcome ally. I ate a bag of chips and two packages of peanuts in the dark, but nothing else, over this long and terrible period, so getting something to eat came to my aid just in the nick of time.

"Get out of this room," flowed out as if someone else spoke. "Get out of this room," and in a jiffy. Zing, my shorts and shirt were on, shoes in hand, car keys in pocket, dead phone in the other, I headed to the door, stopped, panting for breath concerned, full of confusion. "Room key, room key what about the room key, where is it?" Money, I need money for a drive thru, coffee and breakfast sandwich you have to have money. Back in the bowels of the dark room, I struggled to get everything I needed before the door locked behind me. If the click of the clock stopped, time seemed to be going backward. I fumbled, stumbled wanting to break in frustration over such a small issue. Getting a few stark items, became a herculean task. I almost fell onto the bed and right back into a hopeless spiral of despair. Instead I sat on the edge of the bed, took in a deep breath and thought.

Car keys, phone, debit card, room key. Car keys, phone, debit card, room key. Car keys, phone, debit card, room key. Simple enough. Twenty minutes later with, car keys, phone, debit card, room key running through my mind, I whipped the curtains open. BAM, the brightness blasted like an exploding bomb. Not heat, but blinding illumination. Four items. Only four items. One, two, three, four.

Next thing I knew, I made it to my car with the insurmountable paltry items, plugged the phone in and set off for a coffee, and a warm egg, ham, cheese muffin. Yahoo!

I never got there.

On route I made a call to my brother who had been around several of my episodes over the years, one pretty bad in two thousand and six, but nothing compared to this ordeal.

Thank God he answered.

At the sound of his voice the dam burst. Hyperventilating, convulsing tears poured out in a tsunami, so I pulled over, parked, hoping the onslaught would wash by and so I didn't crash into anyone or anything.

"I am here for you, take your time," my brother told me with genuine compassion, the compassion I fully trust.

In between the stammering gibberish, moaning and tears, he told me, "don't worry, I am here for you."

The words I needed to hear. The perfect medicine. With significant effort I pulled myself away from the cliff where the oppressive abyss beckoned me to jump, to fall, to give in. I yanked myself away onto an unstable and slippery slope, but away from the gripping power of despair.

To keep myself from sliding, I shook my head back and forth, back and forth, back and forth in rapid suggestion. I pounded the steering wheel, I bounced in my seat. Much of the conversation I do not remember, but the important issue sticks in my mind as if drilled, staked and bolted to my psyche as a permanent fixture.

"What about the wedding?" he asked

"No problem it is tomorrow at noon, I have a full day to get this under control."

"Oh," he said, "is the wedding on Saturday?"

"No, Friday."

"It is Friday."

"No, it isn't," I told him with complete conviction. The certainty of the day of the week could not be shaken from my resolve. I knew for sure, for sure. Then I started thinking there is a sinister plot going on here, a trick, some type of trick, except not from my brother. No way from him. I fumbled for my phone, struggling for the calendar app, but the tears were back with a vengeance.

"It is okay, don't worry." He told me, but I didn't listen. Panic set in. The calculation of time, logistics, my demented state, plus the sweeping emotions standing at the door of my mind and window of my heart, seemed insurmountable. I felt defeated, desired to give in and give up.

Then he asked, "where are you?"

I knew my location, where I parked, in front of what store, on the very street, but my mind started spinning like a pinwheel blown by a hurricane. I could not answer. My brother waited. He must have heard and felt my struggle to answer. I started mumbling then I said, "Twenty minute, twenty minutes, twenty minutes."

"You are twenty minutes away?"

Twenty minutes I stammered and started rolling. Put the car in first gear and moved, shifted to second and low in behold I found myself on my way to a wedding, without the ability to know if I would crack up and ruin the big day for my beautiful son and his lovely bride.

"Okay you have time, there is time. Take a deep breath."

I sucked in a ravenous breath, and many more than one. Gallons of deep breaths, long, slow steady. In and out up and down. The inhalations brought a flicker of calmness and snapped a bit of sanity in place although tied together in tight knots of worry, fear, regret and shame.

Shit, shit, shit. How could it be Friday, it is not Friday, no way, no way, no way? What if I did not go out for food? If I didn't call my brother?

"Can you make it home? Are you okay to drive?"

I shook my head in the affirmative, up and down, up and down.

"Do you need someone to get you? Are you safe to drive?"

"I am driving."

"Are you safe?"

"I think so, I think so, I think so." I pounded the wheel and shook my head back and forth with fervor trying to get the webs out along with the tears, mumbles and stutters. To make the gibberish go away. No good to show up as a twitching, raving lunatic. Not on this day of all days.

Shit.

With my brother still on the hands-free call, I cried out, "I need clothes, I need clothes, I need clothes."

Here is a confession. Looking back, I should have been wise or sane enough to see the blinking light of concern over my daily routine. For months I only wore shorts and a cotton T-shirt, bare foot except into a grocery store, bank or other establishment where the sign read, NO SHIRT, NO SHOES, NO SERVICE! I left a pair of lace up sneakers in my car just for the occasion, otherwise, no shoes.

This may not seem a big deal except I wore the same shorts and shirt for days on end without taking a shower. Days and days on end. From the fall, through winter jeans and a long sleeve flannel rarely with shoes on, but from late winter through spring, shorts and a thin short-sleeve shirt. Dirty shorts and a stinky T-shirt are the wrong attire for a wedding.

"No problem, I will call home for you." He assured. "I will let them know to set out the clothes. Are you safe to drive?"

"Tell them not to talk to me, don't ask questions, don't ask questions, no questions. I need clothes, I need clothes."

"How far away are now?"

"Fifteen minutes, fifteen."

"I will call for you, just drive safe."

"Okay, okay, okay."

"They all love you and I love you. You are not alone in this."

"I don't want to wreck the wedding," I burst out. "I don't want to ruin the wedding."

"You won't."

Understatement of the century, maybe of all time.

I knew the ceremony would take place at noon on our neighbors' property, only I believed it would be the next day. My mind had difficulty coming to grips with the reality of losing an entire day. Unbelievable. I trust my brother more than words can say, so I rejected my twisted tendency to take time to uncover the mystery, get to the bottom of the conundrum and figure out where the missing link disappeared. No time to dabble. Time was not on my side. I could make it home in one piece, get cleaned up, dressed for the occasion with not much time to spare, so contemplation of this crazy needed to take a back seat, locked up for another day.

As I drove home one of the beautiful perfect seven called. I know we spoke, but for the life of me I cannot remember a word of our communication. Down deep I believe I did not convey any weird or nutty statements.

I lowered my windows so the wind would pelt me with a loud whistling pounding in a hope to snap me into some semblance of normality. I belted out, at the top of my lungs, over and over, La, la la la la la la, as I drove with the best opera voice I could muster. Deep, loud, long, over and over and over.

As I made my way closer, a subtle light of illumination shined with clarity out of nowhere, from a place I could not put a finger on. No clanging symbol rang out or a magical revelation, only a small truth. I needed help. Actual help, professional help. No more hiding and washing over the deep issues I covered up and avoided my whole life. No more could I fake. No going back. I knew I had to hold it together for the next few hours, honor the beautiful nuptials and by all means do not have any outbursts, then I would have to deal with the mental pretzel I found myself twisted and tied in.

A wedding holds a powerful healing balm. Two becoming one, embraces a mystery with gifts able to extinguish darkness and put to death despair, flip the bird to hell and stomp to dust insanity. Seeing the wall to wall smile across the gorgeous face of the second of the seven shined a bright warm light of hope and possibility. The confirmation kiss became sweet icing on the cake of new life with endless optimistic outcomes. Plus, the in-laws are absolutely fantastic, better than great. A lovely, kind, sweet, awesome bride for my son and her incredible family to boot.

Unfathomable grace.

Besides the wonders of pure matrimony, a brand-new daughter and her wonderful family, the Beautiful Perfect Seven were all in one place. I contemplated the last time we were all together, which did not become a good practice in my shaky state, so I put to bed those thoughts, tucked them away for another day and allowed deep love and gratitude to rise to inaccessible heights as a weapon against the bottomless dungeon of mental torment.

It worked. At least until the celebration ended, the bride and groom went off to their honeymoon and all the guests departed.

Then the intervention came.

A plan behind the scenes took place outside my ears, understanding or discernment. After the celebration broke up, I felt a strange euphoria welling through all the cells in my body. From my bare toes to the bald spot on my head. Happiness, glee, anticipation, hope, excitement. Weird, I know. After long painful days in a dark cave under a wet cloud of utter despair with whacked out psychosis, which fired full steam ahead mere hours before, should have extinguished any smiles or excitement. I get it. I cannot explain the shift, except to say exuberance is better than despair hands down, not even a question. Joy feels good, sorrow sucks. Happiness is so much more valuable than grief and hope kicks the ass of dread pure and simple.

I cannot remember the conversations, or the words I spoke after the celebration, probably crazy talk, I cannot remember. I only have a recollection of the feelings, the wonderful feelings. Love. gratitude, joy, anticipation. I came back from the dark cold abyss to a pleasant warm light of freedom, deliverance, a place of normality set in hope, with a deep well of genuine gratitude and appreciation. Then a reasonable request threated to undo me.

The first and fourth of the seven confronted me, bless their hearts. Looking back, I would have done the same. Out of genuine concern, love and worry they talked together, behind the scenes, and formulated a well thought out plan. I do not blame them; in fact, I respect their fortitude, ingenuity, and reasons. How could I not, they are two of the Beautiful Perfect Seven?

They did not confront me nor did they corner me. Out of undeniable compassion, seasoned with wisdom and a few sprinkles of fear, they asked me to go to the hospital for some tests. I think the concern bent toward the possibility of a brain tumor or some other serious physical condition. As a precaution only, they wanted me to get checked out. No sinister plot, just in case, get checked out.

A familiar unwelcome deception started knocking to enter into the lower parts of my guts. Even though I listened with a giddy, submissive open heart, my minded started doing somersaults and back flips. *Shit, they want to lock me up.* They want me to go to a psychiatric facility for a seventy-two-hour lock down or whatever the name.

Not good.

I think, although I cannot remember, most still elutes me, but I believe I started to cry and shared my deep desire and fear about a lockdown. I must have shared this fear out loud, as I can sense a reassurance there would be no intention of committing me. I know I believed at that point, the purpose of going to the hospital was benign. Tests to eliminate any physical condition to explain wild emotional swings, confusion, paranoia and memory loss. At least a week before my breakdown to several weeks after, my memory is all glitched up with empty spots full of fussy disconnected faded parts so I cannot say for sure. All I know is an hour or so later I internally started to freak out.

They drove me to the emergency entrance of the hospital. Since this did not equate to an immediate emergency, they parked, and we walked to the outdoor check-in. Due to the state wide stay at home orders for COVID-19 only one person, the sick person, could go in with a mandatory face mask. I stood there putting on my mask to obediently go in when a police office, probably a security guard, walked up looking at me with a suspicion gaze. I only saw the uniform and the look in his eye. The unblinking stare centered with a sharp focus directly on me and nowhere else. I felt his eyes say, "I am here to take you in boy, lock you up, so don't make any waves or it will be worse for you." HEE, HEE, HEE. Can anyone say paranoia? I did and in spades. From my throat to my belly, electric pulsating fear arched with enough current to make my head light up and burst. Terrorizing fear gripped me, every conspiracy theory on the planet rolled into one bombarded my thoughts. The feeling of being lied to, duped and cheated rose up with a significant fright and flight motivation, but two of the seven were with me, standing right by me, they brought me, they love me and I love them, so I stayed put and did not indulge the onslaught of the hyper verbal arguments ricocheting around my unstable head. They assured me again, I came for tests and nothing else. Even though I believed their assurance, fear and paranoia snapped together like two unbreakable puzzle pieces leaving me between the rock of a padded cell and the hard place of reality to trust those I love. My immediate response went to my long-lived go-to.

Cheating, deception and persuasion.

Who cares if they lock me up, I will talk my way out of it?

It doesn't matter, I would lie through my convincing teeth and persuade with calm conviction, they caught in their traps the wrong person. No way would I open up with honesty regarding my creepy episodes over the previous weeks.

An elaborate intricate imagination, from beginning to end, clicked across my vision in less than a second. Full on conversations, a specific nurse, two orderlies, the room they would lock in me, even the head shrink. I could see them, feel their personalities as I played out a five-sided conversation, all in high definition color and surround sound with the end result being released quickly with thumbs up, smiles and a pat on the back asking me to come back for a visit.

"You never should have been here, but we thoroughly enjoyed our time with you. Come back and see us again sometime."

The security guard with his eye on me turned away and walked off. In the end, my worry proved to be unwarranted, just like so many other times. The man worked for a living, he had a job to do and it did not include escorting me to a padded cell.

An immense relief.

As the sick one who did not choose to get checked out, but submitted to the plan, I felt gratified to enter alone, all by myself. Only the patient could go in.

Sweet.

There is no preparation for going crazy.

I went in with me, myself and I with my mask on, checked in and waited, and waited and waited and waited tapping my toes to the music singing through my soul. Unjustified and unexplainable euphoria rose in me creating an unusual sway in my hips, started the moment I walked into the emergency room. Some abstract rhythm bubbled inside my bones giving me an overwhelming desire to break out in a spontaneous dance. In my guts beautiful melodic tunes began play. Then some external ethereal song, many songs, only I could hear, rang through my mind in perfect time as if a station, set to all my greatest hits ran on loop, commercial free, producing a crescendo of joyful exuberance down in my soul.

I wanted to dance.

I held myself together and did not get up and do a jig in front of the other sickies in the room, but I wanted to. In fact, I used the bathroom several times and let loose. Swinging, swaying, jiving and came out with a fake stoic look on my face holding down a weird spring in my step and went back to waiting, tapping my toes the whole time.

Like six hours of waiting.

Welcome to health care in the richest nation on earth. My first thought went to a government run facility, the DMV or a Social Security office. Cold, bare, unfeeling and dreary. Light colored linoleum floors, low back vinyl chairs, two wide screen TV's, on both sides of the room, and a bunch of waiting. Sitting still and waiting. Hour after hour, switching seats to give my butt cheeks a respite and place to recuperate. I sat with dozens of others. Old and young, rich and poor. Clearly the emergency room waiting area became a stomping ground for the less than ambulatory souls who did not require immediate, lifesaving care. It seemed to be the place for hordes of stable souls wishing or wanting treatment or diagnosis and somehow, I became one. Sure, there were a few who were clearly ailing, and I felt obliged to give up my seat for them, but in the end, no one died or needed to be swished away.

After the sun went down, by hours I went behind closed doors. Blood, urine, and a few other battery of tests. In the end, I needed to go somewhere else to get the imaging of my brain.

Could be a brain tumor ya know.

The last item, the one to determine if I needed to stay overnight, inpatient they called it, turned out to be sitting in a room alone, in front of the kiosk, they rolled in and I waited again until a head shrink from a different city and time zone, I concluded, came on the screen.

Tele health.

As I waited, I prepared. More than preparation, I created a firm detailed plan from beginning to end. I needed whoever blinked on the screen to wash their hands of me with enthusiasm. I used my manipulative powers to make sure I did not have to stay overnight for observation. It turned out to be an easier task than I imagined. Much easier than the elaborate plan I prepared in advance.

I made sure the music playing my favorite tunes settled down to soft background melody and to clamp down the unnatural grin plastered across my face for the last several hours. It turned out I had plenty of time to adjust, settle and move into persuasive sales mode, to close the deal.

At least an hour I sat alone in a six by nine-foot room. The video doc, for some reason did not know I eagerly waited for our long distant therapy session. Three times, very friendly nurses, male and female, fiddled with the kiosk with the same statement. "I am not sure what is taking so long." I did not care, I needed time to prepare for my performance.

The kiosk blinked to life and a forty something shrink came into view. I looked right into the camera, so this far removed distant mind doc would see me eye to eye. I blinked intermittently in a "look normal" effort. Interesting enough, the video doctor looked anywhere but the camera. It did not matter, I held firm with my best effort to appear stable and of sound mind.

If they only knew.

I stated right up front the two issues I convinced myself needed attention. The two I felt certain had to be on the top of the checklist.

I delivered the statement with as much clear, sound minded emphasis as I could muster.

"I have no desire to hurt myself or any others."

A masterful delivery. Pure, simple, and with sober conviction. Gold metal answer from the clinically disturbed who wholeheartedly did not want to stay overnight for observation. My declaration did the trick. The rest of the time went like a breeze. The wide smile I worked to keep hidden, made a couple of unwelcome appearances, but all in all, I did a fantastic job of convincing the holder of the keys to set me free.

A great feeling.

When the screen went blank, back to the "PLEASE WAIT FOR YOUR DOCTOR TO ARRIVE," I opened up and let the music play in quadriphonic sound loud and with a heightened volume. I think it was Old Time Rock-and-Roll, by Bob Seger.

"Just take those old records off the shelf
I'll sit and listen to 'em by myself
Today's music ain't got the same soul
I like that old-time rock 'n' roll."

Ya, ya, ya.

I stood up and let loose with everything I had in me. Hands raised, hips swaying, head bobbing and feet a movin. Awesome, simply awesome, but I still needed to go through one more gate keeper before I got sprung, so a sat like a perfect obedient teacher's pet and waited. Time for celebration would come in due time.

My wait did not take long at all. A short few minutes later. The door opened and an ER doc came in with surgical scrubs wearing a thoroughly bored expression on her face clearly seen even behind the new-fangled and required, facial mask. My first thought went to her countenance. Depression, boredom, un-happy to be here.

As she went through her duties like a rusted robot, I wanted to tell her, "get out now, this job sucks lady," but I held my tongue. I needed to get out more than she did. In the end I thanked her for being an essential worker and bingo, I walked out, free as a bird, with a bouncy spring in my step, swaying to the music in my head.

I should mention, during this time in the hospital and in fact since my mind broke, I did not wear my glasses. I took them off days before and I believed I chucked them in the trash as a vow or more like self-delusion. I had my prescription sunglasses to drive while in my car, but I could not see the faces of anyone around me. So, my freedom came with life changes of my making. Squinting to see up close and a crystal-clear knowledge I needed corrective lenses to get around and maneuver life. I did not get locked up, which is a big deal, a great big deal, plus the unexplainable euphoria zipping through my system helped me douse these blaring undeniable issues.

It did not last very long.

My mind flashed on cylinders I did not know existed. Not only sparks and revving power, but full on brilliant explosions of insight and secret revelations to the mysteries of the universe. I believed I tapped the mother lode of understanding and it felt fantastic. Looking back, it is easy to see, and I should have seen, how odd and incongruent this drastic flip flop of emotion was. More than odd, downright nuts. If there is a clear sign post of imbalance and mental instability, my days of blabbering conversations, memory loss, wailing, moaning, incoherent gibberish to emotional ecstasy in a snap, should have flagged me down and got my attention. But flying high is so good, logical recognition cruises far below the radar.

The amount of whack-a- doodle things I said and did from the breakdown until the seven went back to their lives are too many to recount and most I feel in memory with disgust, regret and shame. My poor children. If I could go back and have a re-due, I would in a minute, but I trust them and believe in their strength and resiliency. I also believe and have confidence they may come to me and ask, or want to talk about their perceptions or concerns, during this period, and my heart is an open book to them.

When you zip across galaxies of understanding, sleep becomes a hindrance. At least in my case. Out of ignorance, denial or flat out selfish desire to feel great, I slept very little after I got released as a free bird from the hospital. This turns out to not be a conscious decision. More of a stupid oversight.

As an example, I arrived at my house from the ER late, maybe midnight and I went to bed. At one thirty, an hour and a half later, I woke up, bright eyed and bushy tailed. Cloud nine may be a better expression. Either way, I felt refreshed, energetic and raring to go. By the time midnight rolled around again, I felt a strange energy to keep going, so I did until early afternoon the next day. I took a two-hour nap and up again with a bouncing spring in my step.

After the week I went through I should have been conscious enough to realize the severity of the unhealthy imbalance that grabbed ahold of me. The abnormal evil disturbing emotional swings from crushing-low to ultra-high should have been a bright flashing clue.

I have no excuse.

At the time I could not see. Plus, the highs are so good, so powerful, they extinguish discernment or any desire for reflection. Plus, they wash worry and concern right down the drain with a vengeance.

Since then, I see part of my path to continual stability requires consistent bouts of prolonged rest and sleep. If I do not sleep the crazy stands at the door with a slight tapping until the bell rings and I find myself down the rabbit hole of the utter ridiculous. Even though it may be days until the keepers of the straight jacket even begin to turn their eye in my direction, I will start rolling on the tracks of a runaway train, and no matter how nice the ride seems, the end is destruction and despair, plus the path back runs the gambit of an ugly, long, hard struggle and painful reflection.

Resting my body and mind in a consistent pattern is one of the arrows I hold in my new found quiver to hit the bullseye I long for.

Normality, balance and emotional stability.

I understand many people have trouble with insomnia and I feel for them, but I have not struggled with those problems. The instant I hit the pillow I am lights out. My entire life has been this way. I can almost fall asleep, standing up. My problem falls to the other end of the spectrum. The lack of or need for, or at least the thought of no need for sleep. This idea is the enemy of normality and a stable healthy existence.

It took me five decades to figure out this little morsel of truth.

The embryonic understanding did not come easy. Hell, unleashed on me before I could agree with what the entire world seems to know. "Get enough sleep. It is unhealthy not to rest. Sleep is important."

I should have gotten the clue and woke up to the reality. Instead I mentally broke apart, and it did not get put back together with a few hours of REM infused sleep. Delusion, deception, anxiety, crazy talk, sprinkled with nutty thoughts and weird actions came first. If you sleep only an hour or four over a three-day period, euphoria may set in, but the end comes with horrible hallucinations and a long road back home. The tradeoff is not worth it.

Trust me.

Two days of buzzing with elations turned on a dime and mixed together in the crushing mush of emotional upheaval and tweaked understanding, then started to spin out of control. The tears were back and stronger than ever along with twitching, shaking, some verbal stutters, plus a massive amount of messed up ideas sweeping through my mind turning my internal compass anywhere but true north.

Literally I felt undone, torn to mental shreds.

I had times of anxiety in my life, but those felt like a soft warm breeze compared to the full body slam of this physical and mental bombast of arching electric shocks with the end result of sinister unease unleashed through every part of me. Head to toe. Every pore, every nerve ending, each synapse in my brain, turned to overload with no signs of relenting. In fact, the opposite seemed to be the case. More, more, more, faster and faster. Looking back my best explanation is a whirl-a-wheel playground spinner. Once you get on, you cannot get off, especially when it picks up speed. I felt as if the anxious twirl in me would never stop while it smirked in my face, picking up with twirling power and frightening velocity.

As bad as crippling depression may seem to be, worse is the over enthusiastic declaration of the poker hand in this realm. No way to tell as both suck the big one to the absolute max. Depression and rocketing anxiety on a balancing scale, tilting to one side or the other, could surely give a sober individual a moment for pause, but mental health issues do not stand erect on a balancing scale, so the one with more power and or, the more debilitating, stand outside the judge's corner to decide. Each raise up and erect themselves on their own power with interwoven sneaky outward influences and internal weaknesses. Flip a coin and chose. It might be head comes up on both sides and you will find yourself in a quandary, an isolated helpless state. Welcome to the club. Either way, there is no way to turn off or shut down with a thought or simplistic hope, unworldly, unexplainable, depression or hyper euphoric fly to the stars whacked out fantasy, both hold the same power with the same end game.

Destruction of the soul.

Set your smiling face to dancing on manic overload, or bury your head in the sand in crushing despair, both are equal. One comes with a smile, the other with a defeated frown, but the end result remains the same.

A real-world quandary.

Forget-about-it.

Depression crinkles your guts into a compact ball with orders to sleep an inconsolable amount of time as an isolated temporary escape until you open your eyes again. Then real true blue, physical anxiety produces a terrible and overwhelming need to scream your head off, run away, with the knowledge neither will do any good, so you suffer wanting to scream and run from whole-body buzzing pointed directly against your spirit with tormenting pulses through each and every nerve cell cramping down to make you the worst ineffective and worthless being.

For some unknown reason I chose a weird response, as an abnormal reaction to this unknown enemy I never tumble with before. I do not hold any place of recognition or desire for inclusion in a hero's memorial or honored with some hidden acceptance. On the contrary, I know, am fully convinced, absolutely aware, and downright humiliated to discern how far off the mark I flung my heartfelt and faithful arrows short, into the dirt as useless ineffective toothpicks against the stalwart oppressor.

Just one of billions across the planet, solar system, galaxies, far past and over many unseen centuries into oblivion, and then some. Small and tiny, but at the same time more valuable than the most precious metal or beating heart. Greater and more magnificent, far past worth and value. All in one tiny blink of specks and dust.

Great and Marvelous are HIS ways. Just and True is the creator almighty.

Who is the King of Saints?

A profound question.

As a supersonic, eternal and most valuable life form, just as all are, how is it at the same moment, every one of us bolt in billions of different directions? I conclude the keeper of majestic profound and unimaginable power holds us together and speaks to each of us our profound significant and individual value.

I could be wrong, but hang in there as I unfold a few wild and crazy moments. In the end you can burn this, outlaw this, or become a pacifist and allow these simple, twisted typed words to fall into the dust heap.

Either way I hope you may open up and take the ride.

Zing, Zing, Zing. Get on board.

I do not attempt to, or hold any true and sincere place of dignity. On the contrary, I understand fully I do not contain any real or cognitive understanding, with confirmation as a secret weapon to abolish the potent and thoroughly defeated rubbery sling shots unable to penetrate my child like shield.

I stand alone. A simple creature, living between self-sacrifice, self-abasement and fleeting, but powerful hope.

Denial and gratification.

Two sides of the coin of life. The twisted equation.

What to do?

The deceitful, lying, downright quandary of life or better said, this horrifying existence.

They bounced off, fall to the ground and revealed themselves as worthless and thoroughly ineffective BB shots. Simple low velocity mineral infused pellets.

An unloaded false enemy.

BINGO.

My battled turned out to be internal and not from some powerful unseen foe on the outside. The revelation brought with it a smooth comfort, along with a rocky sharp personal attack. Many deceptive tracks leading in different directions all containing a tiny bit of truth, lead me further away, anywhere but stability, until they circled back, and I found parts of a sound mind.

It did not come easily or by a path I would give directions to. DO NOT ENTER SIGNS should be posted in triplicate stating THIS IS THE WRONG WAY. A treacherous road no one should take. No way to go back and try another route to avoid the pitfalls. Sometimes you have to travail through the quagmire of delusion to arrive in one piece at a destination of partial normality with parts of an actual clear mind.

One suggestion I can give with complete conviction, is to NOT, DO NOT, state, or speak the wild and crazy things ricocheting across your mind, no matter how brilliant they may seem. The other is to not share the weird things which seem important. I did with a fervor and looking back I know this is not good. Actually, words ideas, thoughts, philosophies and the tiny little quirks have negative value and are counterproductive.

Here is an illustration.

The papers

I wrote many specific notes, printed certain pictures, copied song lyrics, poems, a few scriptures. Day by day I accumulated these, folded them and titled each for easy access. By the end I had a thick stack of paper each holding a specific value to my heart and mind. For a reason I cannot explain, I held an unhealthy need to carry these with me at all times. I touched them without pulling them out and a genuine calm comfort flowed. A wad of paper in my pocket as a security blanket.

My Binky.

Like I said, "WEIRD."

I have difficulty remembering in whose presence or how many times I pulled them out, shuffled through and read or showed the papers off. The thought leaves me with nothing less than complete pitiful embarrassment. I still have the sheets although without a need or desire to touch or carry them around.

Got to be thankful for small miracles.

Here is the list of the titles and a brief explanation from the first to the last.

The note–the seventh of the beautiful seven wrote a note as a first grader to me. I cherish it more than I can say. Misspelling and all.

RBYBW–Red, brown, yellow, black and white, all are precious in HIS sight. I wrote out the whole song. Jesus loves the little children.

New Friend – I met a man in the grocery store and somehow believed we would become best friends.

Numbers Six– "The Lord turn his face toward you and gives you peace."

Silence–The art of silence and the value in a vow of silence.

The Screen Door–Emotions are like waves of the ocean, don't fight, let them flow and settle.

Little Boy–Come they told me Pa rum pump um pum, A newborn king to see, Pa rum pum pum

1970s–pictures of memories when I grew up.

The Words–Philippians 4:8, 2 Corinthians 10:5, Matthew 6:33, Colossians 3:2, James 4:7.

EQ–List of Emotional Quotient I resonated with.

Some Kind of Crazy–Highlights from a book I read from a man I respect.

The Resonator–A blogger who stated, "my heart is racing. An imaginary band tightens around my chest. I want to scream." It goes on for four paragraphs. I feel and resonate with each word.

The Word and Sleep–Scriptures on rest and sleep.

Stable Life–A list such as exercise, eat well, rest, gratitude, hygiene.

Cover–A picture of the cover of the novel I wrote.

The numbers–Data and stats on COVID-19 infections and deaths by age.

Manic–A list of the risk-taking decisions I made throughout my manic life. A very long list.

The Corruption - A list of all the religious influence I corrupted myself under, from Catholic, Evangelical, Pentecostal, anti-Baptist, to reformed and gobs and gobs of others. The list went on for two pages. I blame myself. GOD HELP ME?

The Seven–A picture of the beautiful perfect seven. So good, so outstanding. A powerful stabilizing force and undeserved gift from GOD.

These Eight and a half by eleven folded sheets of plain every day paper went with me everywhere I went and seemed to give me a bit of peace, but they did not stop the crazy talk. Although I tried with diligence and conviction, I could not keep myself from puking out the most farfetched, lunacy and crack pot philosophies. I spouted the worst rambling unstable diatribes all the while I told myself to shut up.

I did not listen to myself.

A stumbling drunk, on an acid trip, after smoking three pipe loads of potent weed, would have sounded more sober and sound minded.

Crap.

Oddly enough when I shared my screwed-up thoughts about all matter of strange things, I did not feel the pounding anxiety, so, by the power of some silent hidden protection mechanism, I poured forth, with no inhabitations. Then my recollection drifted back to a sure clear commitment I made to myself, but forgot when the euphoria and epilation made me bounce with transformative joy on the balls of my feet. With major ups and down I let the recollection speak volumes and clarity.

I need professional help! I need a diagnosis and a proper treatment plan!

Several times a day as I battled against an unseen foe, fact-based discernment pounded forth to seek help and fast. I knew I needed to get a grip. Beside the crazy talk, two issues, shined like a cruel spotlight on my very existence. Delusions and My Tongue, both were bad.

Worse than bad.

Delusions

I mentioned how I went online and found all the mind doctors and "Professionals" pitching their wares. I only searched for those with a PHD. I passed by all the marriage and family counselors (MFC). Counseling did not even scrape the bottom of the barrel of the massive iceberg I found myself crushed under. No need to scratch the surface. I needed down in the dirt, under the mud, bulldozers to chisel out the unmovable boulders I erected in my psyche. I needed a true blue, skilled, effective, trained, demolition crew to tear up my faulty infrastructure and make plans to rebuild from the ground up on a sure foundation. A counselor did not fit the bill. Those with degrees seemed to be the place to find a diagnosis and a sound treatment plan. A good thought. A reasonable assumption.

Nope.

It took me a fair amount of time, through personal experience, to understand the reality of mental health care service and treatment in this new millennium in the United States of America.

The good old USA.

Before I did, I had the worse, terrifying close call with the lie and fierce enemy of my soul and thank God for the seven being nearby to keep me grounded in reality and from going off the cliff into a horrifying icy valley of total insanity.

Here is what happened.

I lined up my call list with many Phycologists and the one Psychiatrist nearby. Due to my conviction of how screwed up I found myself twisted in multiple unbreakable knots, the only one in town who could prescribe potent mind-altering medications, seemed the prudent first choice to call and book an appointment. Makes sense. Logical and well thought out. I thought so, and then the fucking lie pounded with ferocious deceptive power for at least three hours.

No kidding.

I started in the late morning calling and by early afternoon I made no progress and boiled with the worst frustration all the while feeling I had been nailed and spike to a bout of indescribable terrible anxiety. The worst type bar none. Call them uneven straight lines fuzzy detached unconnected particles with only a few contained elements, but somehow turned sideways on their heads in a multi colored kaleidoscope with unfocused vision as blobs and you might come close to seeing the light only to miss the mark in an undeniable diluted experience.

Join the club.

The anxiety started slow, after an hour or so, of working the phone to talk with someone, and book and appointment. During this time, I heard the very faint whisper of the lie.

This is not real, nothing is real, give up.

I have a bit of tenacity in me, and stupidity, so I spend several more hours calling the same number, pushing every button, winding up where I started out over and over again, but with life gripping crippling delusion.

The anxiety became unbearable. Forget the Psychiatrist I need a padded cell. Lock me up and pump drugs in me to knock me out. I literally felt my entire body shaking from every nerve ending with the one purpose to make my head blow off in a preordained explosion.

Some abnormal desires I battled against, included pounding my phone to tiny bits, picking my desk up, flipping it over and throwing it against the wall, were only two of the wild cat emotions running at warp speed through me. Breaking windows, slamming doors and a couple others rose their ugly distorted faces into my eyesight, but screaming my head off won first place without a close runner up.

The Psychiatrists office, I will call, "The Great Head Shrink of Northern California," has the worse, absolutely the worst, phone system bar none. Are you kidding me? People going nuts, SHOULD NOT BE sent through an endless rabbit hole of a voice prompted phone tree, but I do not run the great head shrink's office so there you go.

Then the volume and speed of the lie increased to a place I could not overcome or put back into the box. Out in the open, playing like an out of tune screeching fiddle.

THIS PROVE NOTHING IS REAL. WHAT MORE DO YOU NEED TO SEE? PULL THE STRING, PULL IT NOW AND YOU WILL GO TO WHERE YOU REALLY EXIST.

On and on and on this clanging, temptation continued with unstopping vengeance as I paced back-and-forth twitching like a palsy-stricken nut ball. I battled with the best verbal come back I could muster. I sat down at times taking in massive breaths. I literally found against words in my head, by speaking out loud. I went to the head shrinks website, pointing my finger at the phone number as a winning argument.

IT IS NOT REAL, NONE OF THIS IS REAL, PULL THE STRING, ONCE AND FOR ALL.

The instant I went from delusion to stammering less than coherent verbal connection, I scribbled down the phone number on a tiny scrap of paper and stumbled my way for outside help.

The first and fourth of the seven, yes, the two who asked me to get tests done, where together talking, a beautiful wonderful sight I now see clearly. On that day, I walked blind, deaf and dumb, off my proverbial rocker, stammering, unstable crazy boy, so I could not appreciate their unfathomable value. But now I do with inexpressible gratitude.

Physically twitching, wanting scream at the top of my lungs and about to burst into and endless ocean of tears, I laid the scribbled note down. I cannot fully recollect the stuttering words, only, "I need help."

I spent hours, wrestling a phone system, and battling the lie and found myself in a state of horrible delusion. The fourth of the seven got through, with the appointment scheduler in a matter of minutes, handed me the phone and bingo I am in.

What the hell.

After I booked an appointment for "Diagnosis," with the all-important "treatment plan," I spouted out, with a jitter and a bit of a cracking stumble in my voice.

It went something like this.

"Thank you for your service, I appreciate you helping me set an appointment. I am thankful to you, but if you do not mind, can I make a suggestion?" Without waiting for a response, I pressed full speed ahead. "I get the first part of your voice prompt system getting out of the way for liability purposes, the big one. If this is an emergency hang up and call 911. Seems right, good in fact, but the next words should be, if you need to speak with someone press one or for goodness' sake, PRESS ZERO. Your phone system needs to be overhauled, revamped. Just a suggestion, but who am? I understand I am only a prospective nut job client, and I did not hear a request or guidance to a suggestion box, so I am suggesting you have whoever deals with your phone system and the voice prompts, make a few changes."

Just a suggestion.

Then I went through the list, best as I can recall in my detached whole hearted recollection, which may be a bit skewed. I feel and sense through reminiscence, my words came across with a humble, subservient tone. Not haughty, arrogant or with a judgmental emphasis on my words or hidden critical agenda behind my intension.

I said. "Having to go through nine prompts is aggravating and may cause struggles worse than the reason for the call." I spirted out, from memory of my experience. "Billing press one. Prescription refill two. Press three if you would like to leave a message for your therapist. Four if you have an insurance matter. Five if you need to reschedule your appointment. Six, seven, eight and then nine, if you need to speak with someone please wait on the line."

I found myself speaking some of my crazy thoughts to a complete stranger who most likely could do nothing, but I continued unwavering.

"And then when you get to the end to wait to speak with a real person, nothing, absolutely nothing, only white noise. I pressed zero multiple times and again, nothing, nothing. Your system needs a compassionate update."

Shame and humiliation still hold the power to poke a red-hot dagger into my memory with painful heat at the thought. The worst is the fact the fourth of the seven, who got through on the line and brought the open phone to me so I could make my coveted appointment, listened and watched as I spit out my screwed-up diatribe on clerical improvements I somehow knew were extremely important changes needing to take place immediately.

Shit.

Seeing my daughter, the greatest of great, in my minds view, sitting and listening, observing me, puking my delusional guts out, threatens to undo the progress I made since that fateful, painful time. But as I mentioned, the Beautiful Perfect Seven, keep me grounded and give me hope.

It helps me to skip around a bit before as I unfold the details I experienced, the place where the light of stable reality left me alone in a cold, black abyss, gasping, clawing in nothingness, detached on an overload of heart stopping anxiety.

Melodramatic? Could be or not in the slightest. Over exaggerated? Far from my view point. I will freely express written words may appear inept to describe the, oh let me see, the fucking devastating horror.

If an unseen force ripped my scalp off and dug into my brain with sharpened talons to tear apart every mustard seed of faith and each embryonic particle of hope I still contain, I would not be scratching the surface to accurately convey the power of the clamping forceful grip of the evil attacking my actual existence.

Well then, words might contain a powerful descriptive potency.

Maybe I am wrong.

Who cares?

Thank God I made it to the place of stepping on the solid yellow brick road of possibility to getting help, but I needed to go through a step by step, painful process. First make a connection over the phone line, then, talking to a real-life person giving me a booked appointment, on the calendar to see a real Bonafede head shrink with all the pedigrees, certificates and diplomas.

My elation lasted for an hour or two, then the sweeping anxiety grabbed me by the throat and would not let go.

I need to turn back the clock a few degrees and explain how I lost grip on reality, fighting against my logic as I battled with all my heart against the unemotional, obscure digital terrible phone system. I will confirm I lost the battle for a few hours, although I fought like a champ and in the end found my salvation in confession to two of the beautiful seven.

After I pushed each one of the dials on the key pad over and over again, waited, hung up and started again to make connection, the lie slithered in with a slimy sneaky mocking grin.

I listened at least four times through all nine prompts and listened to the endless white noise with a hope in my heart. I took in with conviction, long deep breaths as no one came on the line, battling against detachment from reality.

I went through the phone tree over and over and over as an obedient prospective childlike client to be, I waited and waited and then I waited more. Pressed all the buttons and waited again. If they had some music playing, I might have waited longer, but no. Not a peep, crackle, not even the smallest amount of static. Only nothingness, blank air, without even the slightest sound.

Then the Lie took over and broke through to uproot the paper-thin connection I held to sanity as I listened and waited for a real person to come on the line while I heard, "This is not real. You need to finally give in and you will be where you really exist. Give up and give in."

This voice tempted me while I listened to the phone tree which sounded something like this. If... you... need... to... speak... with a billing... specialist...... please press.... five... Very irritating, frustrating and downright spooky.

I pressed the other prompts, more than once. It feels like a dozen times. Looking back, I should have stopped, and found people who loved me sooner. The frustration in me rose to heights I have never experienced as my mind battled against the Lie bringing me to the brink with the worst buzzing anxiety.

In the same power of the crippling depression I went through in my early twenties, this painful experience held an ability to suck all hope miles and an arm length from the minutest amount of peace. Anxiety sucks, in a way words cannot describe. It is as if an evil outside force stuck an electric probe right into my chest with an ultra-intense voltage meter turned to overload.

I feared I would physically burst, come apart in a bloody mess.

At that point the euphoria I experienced at the hospital left, and anxiety, paranoia and delusion grabbed a hold with a sickening squeeze. The tears were back attached with an inability to sit still.

Horrible.

During my time of searching for professional help, three of the seven from out of down remained for an extended period. The stay at home orders, working remotely, due to COVID-19, became a sweet gift, at least to me. Better than wonderful having them back home and for more than a couple of days, but I blew it and opened my screwed-up thoughts and twisted philosophies.

A huge mistake.

I knew I needed to open wide in this written talk therapy, and now I find myself unable to turn back. I unknowingly let out a sure pure delusion and downright slimy deception holding an undeserved power over me for more years than I can calculate. I have only spoke of this to one other human being in a far distance place and I do not want to relive the experience as I quiver now under the heavyweight of my slip up. I could go back and press the delete key several times, wash my slip up away and keep meandering down the lonely road keeping up my messed-up ways, but I have come too far to backtrack.

The String.

Pull the string.

A teeny bopper statement, out of nowhere meaning absolutely nothing, until the context comes to the surface and in the end may appear as a nothing burger. Only, all my sinews, enzymes, brain cells, emotions, each and every nerve ending spring with unexplainable electric currents through my body, plus the less or more important recognition of this plight we all as HUMAN BEINGS live under, with the true death sentence, meaning we all will die (ONE DAY), throws a lightning fast slow curving, knuckle ball over the plate of my unstable sanity.

I could live in (DENIAL) as the scriptures teaches. Or I could bend and cave, twist and fall into a penitent position and open up with a whole hearted position and not deny myself.

Is there a balancing scale to give me the answer?

Of course, there is, but it comes from both sides. The new-fangled teaching of the followers of JESUS CHRIST stating without repentance, clear acknowledgment in false teaching with unwavering and absolute conviction, "DO NOT LIVE IN DENIAL."

Yikety Yak, DON'T come back.

The Lord Jesus Christ, Lamb of God, maker of all seen and unseen, said clear and with no inhabitation, "DENY YOURSELF, PICK UP YOUR CROSS DAILY and FOLLOW ME!"

Which path should we go down? What should we do?

Follow an unproven therapy based, well-intentioned, although, lacking, behind unproven philosophy or the real confirmable substance, in a small warm emotional, feel good persuasive declaration containing the slightest bit of actual truth, or the big, immense words, ringing across the cosmos, overlooked as an ancient unheard whisper. The perfectly in tune crescendo echoing from centuries gone by and billions of souls who, lived, breathed, hoped, dreamed, struggle, desired, risked, rested and lived under the most astounding choice.

Deny yourself.

Walk in humility and believe in the unseen and unexplainable with the ringing words, "DENY YOURSELF."

Pick or choose, we all have free will and no lightning bolts will strike us down, but the choice holds many powerful cards.

I choose to spill my guts. Tick, Tick, Tick, Tap, Tap, Tap, on an English language keys board on a battery-operated device with an ability to connect hook up and pull down the world wide web, outdoors at times, but mostly in a cloistered dark room to get out and shine a light against the bright dark concealed anchor of the Lie.

An odd, unusual, but sneaky and influential statement.

Pull the string. Pull it now.

It should be easy, simple, in fact to overlook and send this crazy statement to the dust heap of the RIDICULOUS. "ELEMETARY my DEAR WATSON," in fact, but this is not fiction. Well on the other hand, the lie, tied to the underlining, rusty, corrugated chain, with the tempting words to, "PULL the STRING," connects with a two-pronged threat.

Mental weakness and a regretful belief in the illogical.

I mentioned how at times, out of the blue I will hear an unconnected statement and flash to dozens of life experiences, song lyrics, historical events, stories, mathematical equations and scientific discoveries and then hallucinations flip flop around in my head.

Mostly it comes down to a corner of the eye sense I feel more than I see. Just outside my peripheral vision. When I turn or adjust my sight, nothing is there. The best description I can give is the curly ques. The small black squiggles you see behind close lids on a sunny day. Those small twisty thin hairs you can look beyond and not see or focus in on and bingo there they are floating around. Clear, but irritating when you look directly at them. When you focus on one or a clump, they move out of sight. Down to the left, up to the right, whatever. This is the best analogy I can use as a description to bring confirmation.

I know down to my core, THE STRING, is an illusion, and a messed-up delusion. Only problem the lie comes with teeth in a tricky soft whisper in the ear of my mind.

Reach out, pinch an unseen, green and gold string, and find release from this unexplainable and downright incredible existence, with the sure clear hope I will arrive where I actually exist. All I need to do is just pluck an intangible, just outside my physical sight, waiving in the breeze of craziness with a never-ending constant flapping request of an invisible string. Mostly, and at different times, years and more, this delusion remained dormant. I believe it is because of the miracle of the Beautiful Seven, although it raised its ugly head into my noggin many, many times, which thank God I did not cave in and reach out.

This is crazy, illogical, I understand. The invisible does not have colors for one. There is no string, for another, but the lie comes with a seductive tempting allure, as if it has given me some gift or insight, or message from a different realm.

Here is an obvious fact. I am NO genius, not even close. I do not speak a foreign language; I tried several and utterly failed. When I travel overseas, I point, smile and point again. Whatever they say in their foreign tongue does not influence me and I hope they find joy in mocking my ignorance. Joy is one of the top line important emotions, even if it comes at my expense.

Especially if it does.

Not saying I am a clown, only less than regal.

As I understand I have no aptitude for other languages, I can also state as a matter of fact, I do not understand algebra, let alone any higher math. I cannot do a puzzle for the life of me. I tried to read about quantum theory and quantum mechanics, energy, gravity, particles of light, and ZING, right over my head sending nauseating waves of confusion through my guts. I have no ability to build a house, do plumbing, repair an automobile, play a musical instrument, read or understand the language of computer programming, pass a class in a school room, just to name a few.

I have no qualms with the areas I lack talent or ability. I have never lost sleep, or fought against areas where I have no gift. I have seen other people work their knuckles to the bone trying to learn a skill they have limited strength toward, mostly because the gifts of others made them feel good, I think, and it brings me sadness seeing them struggle to be something other than where their natural talents flow.

I appreciate the talents and gifts of musicians. I cannot sing in tune for the most part and struggle to play more than a few notes on any instrument, but I have received more blessing and true gratification from listening to music than maybe any other part of life except water. In a few days, without water you die, and not a nice peaceful death. Breath, sight, ability to hear, touch, walk, love and on and on, go on the top of the list, no question. Food, for sure, are you kidding me, Wowee, so much with so many flavors and most come from seeds grown right out of the ground, cooked, seasoned, mixed together, turned into a meal with names rooted in nationalities. Chinese, Italian, Mexican, French, Greek.

Breakfast, lunch, dinner, plus dessert and snacks. Factory made snacks, Corporate grown vegetables, fruits. HOLY COW. All tasty and so plentiful, at least in the speck of the universe I find myself currently planted.

Interesting there is no United States of America food. Let's not go there. I would hate to go down a rambling hole with no way out. Safe to say this country in not a nationality, more of a conglomeration and a wild experiment. A place you can find all the other national foods in almost any nook and cranny from coast to coast. But allow me to shift back to music as it illustrates where I am heading in this rolling drawn out explanation to the lie beseeching me to PULL the STRING.

I appreciate almost all music and love more than many forms and it is not worth counting all the while I lack gift and talent to play anything. Music holds a power beyond description, and yet comes from seven notes, give or take, creating billions of songs, instrumentals, symphonies, almost uncountable, out of seven notes, with an endless supply in the vault of inspiration hidden until they come forth from a magical place of inspiration.

Seven notes.

What about language?

As I mentioned I only speak English but not every word, nor do I know how many exist.

Twenty-six letters in the English language making available multitudes of words which are spun together into sentences, paragraphs, complete bound books. Endless written stories, history, teachings, not to mention all the spoken words, pod casts, talking, preaching, arguing.

Twenty-six letters.

Then the new bright and shiny one.

Ones and Zeros in the language of computers creating the most fantastic technologies with more content than anyone could comprehend in fifty lifetimes, all at the fingertips of cre-ators made up of flesh, blood, bone, fat and muscle. Megabytes used to be the thing, then gigs, now it is terabytes for less money than a simple calculator cost when I walked around as a young wiper-snapper. Imagine all the clouds, these server warehouses, storing and backing up every, tweet, thumbs up, uploaded pictures, downloaded or streamed videos all from a ONE and ZERO.

A great and majestic new world.

Makes me think of the trillions of stars across countless gal-axies, or all the sand on every seashore, not to mention all the unique snowflakes and individual rain drops, fallen over centuries. One-part hydrogen two parts oxygen. Two to one holding life sustaining power.

And then along comes movies. Sound, story, visual, all together with one intent, speak a message. Okay, entertainment, but mostly it is to create emotion. Laugher, tears, or fears.

I had a delusion in my mid-teens. I believed music contained hidden messages I needed to unravel, interpret and calculate.

This is not, play Hotel California backwards and hear a secret message. That urban legend inserted satanic underpinnings; my delusion became more sinister than an overt demonic message from hell.

NONE OF THIS IS REAL.

Like a secret agent, I spied out record stores. Big and small. Old and new. These stores do not exist anymore except to sell used records, anyhow, I spent hours alone, touching, feeling, reading, looking for the message I needed to answer this screwed up delusion. I had this tweaked idea the message I sought hid in plain sight through the music and also internally in the actual vinyl records themselves.

Bad deal. Can you say "Twilight Zone?"

Interesting enough going to these places made me feel good, and I met an incredible group of music enthusiasts. I would rub my fingers along the spines, stop and investigate. Big band,

Jazz, Country, Folk, Fifties Rockabilly, late Sixties (now called Classic) Rock, Psychedelic, Easy Listening.

But not Disco. Not Disco. Except Donna Summer. Are you kidding she is so beautiful? But the rest of disco?

Forget-about-it.

I realize I can, without much effort, be imbecilic, also I have slight spurts of brilliance, but all in all I know, I lean in the direction of average and less than extraordinary. On the other hand, I have this highbrow belief every living creature holds a genuine spark of divinity with significant value.

A bit of a quandary

I held an unreal, unhealthy obsession toward an esoteric obscure secret message I convinced myself where hidden in the music, lyrics, and vinyl itself, (the actual circular disc) of produced music from the fifties to the mid-seventies. SECRET, DON'T YA KNOW, I needed to find and decipher and "ALL MY DREAMS WOULD COME TRUE."

A devious crock of shit.

A truly screwed up issue. The need to find the secret message in music left me in what seems to be the blink of a second. No kiss good bye or Bon voyage, truly. As I look back, I do not dig too deep, I only enjoy, oh, what is it called? Twenty-twenty insight with false clarity and years of hindsight shining with a cloudy bit of bright illumination, excuse and the volatile uprooting transition outside my control, as the reason. But a worse and more powerful obsession, started to churn until it came in like a dark frozen flood. More on that slimy despicable INTERLOPER at another time.

First let me highlight the illumination, excuse and transition.

The Illumination.

I had mental issues from a very young age. Hands down, no questioned asked. I blame no one, only an undeniable fact. I did my best. Well, I lied, cheated, stole, faked, manipulated, abdicated, bobbed and weaved and mocked to keep from dealing with the rotting skeleton in the room. This did not become a cure, only a cover up.

Excuse.

I was only a kid back than for crying out-load. Are you kidding me? Have some grace. I am not a kid anymore, although I totally feel young, fit, thin, shiny, until I look in the mirror. What in the world, but back then I was a skinny, bouncy teenager?

Nice excuse, huh?

Transition.

From fourteen years of age, until eighteen, I found myself uprooted and moved, let me count... Hold on, I am tapping my fingers and I do not count well.

Many times.

From the Silicon Valley to the beach south of Santa Cruz. Six months later, back to the Silicon Valley for six months and then to the outskirts of Minneapolis in the land of ten thousand lakes for a year. Oops, back to the Silicon Valley again to a rental on the street I grew up on only to move six months later across the valley. Then a year later, welcome to Sacramento California the state capital, and then twenty mile south to the sticks, where I became an adult. Or at least I turned eighteen.

Then my parents moved back again to the land of ten thousand lakes.

I did not go.

It turned out to be a wonderful gift and the worst curse all wrapped in one.

The transition of moving like a beggar vagabond, punched the weird belief, MUSIC HOLDS THE ANSWER, right in the face, knocking out the creepy obsession.

BINGO.

I found myself set free.

But as I mentioned, crippling depression took over for an unholy season, which happened a few years after becoming an "ADULT." The sneaking, creeping lie came in using several tools. Many twisted lies, disgusting and despicable lies in full force all at once from all over, all around me. An onslaught. Not the big one, but many, off the wall and from different directions as a strategic and fierce battle. From all sides and from every conceivable angle. I made an effort to hold some of my shields as a defensive mechanism. The ones which proved valid many times, backed with some persuasive fanaticism and found myself utterly wiped out, down for the count, but I was not out. On the contrary, I suffered with unending gut punches of depression. Consistent pounding whenever I found myself AWAKE, so I slept sixteen to eighteen hours a day for months on end, then I punched back and found myself on my wobbly knees, until I stood on shaky feet with polluted air in my lungs, gasping for a glimmer of hope to get out of the horrific damp lifeless dungeon of life sucking depression.

More on that surreal experience later, I need to get through with the lie to PULL the STRING.

Took me a while to get here, but hey, I did give a disclaimer.

I have a traveling bone and rambling mind.

After many months of suffering, I moved to a life of depression free living, health, success, some say blessing, and I guess that is right. Externally for sure. Stuff, family, friends, opportunities, but internally where the rubber meets the road, a slight bubbling rumbled and rattled tapping with a familiar threat in the form of psychosis, lingered with accusation and desire to get in and take over.

I compensated and lived the most ridicules manic existence to stave off the evil.

Up, up and away.

For three decades, I existed in a nonstop frenzy. All in, and fast. Lightning fast, with only a few downward spins, which only lasted a week at a time, until snap, crackle, pop, I got on my bouncy legs and, ZING, got busy.

Really busy.

The overcoming way.

The more I poured out myself the more I flew higher and higher, but I had no parachute.

As I ran several businesses, raised the beautiful seven, bought properties, did the grocery shopping, listened to the problems of others, planned vacations and so much more, I had three crutches I leaned on to keep myself up in a false state of stability.

Let's be clear, with no question, I lived with three crutches.

Unstable branches, rickety pieces, throw away materials unable to hold up the smallest of souls. I leaned hard, and I found myself upright up for a season, applying pressure to keep me normal until I fell apart.

Religious Fanaticism. Political Information, and Story.

I will leave off the first two for another time.

Story in the form of books and film.

I listened to hundreds of books on tape. No exaggeration. Mostly fiction, and a good deal of nonfiction. I love story. I believe story to be the true universal part of the human experience which taps directly into, and triggers all the fullness of our emotions, happy or sad, joy or fear, in a profound unexplainable way. Like the story or hate it, no denying the power. You cannot be the same after hearing, listening to, reading or watching a great story.

Written words allow your imagination to soar to realms with sweet awesome power.

Movies, Films, Cinema, Television, takes story to a different level. A dimension, some say takes away the personal imagination, but let's be clear, adds a visual aspect from a collaborative group of professionals, plus sound, both spoken and background.

That being said, I have also watched hundreds, no kidding, of movies and television shows.

Decades before, I lived with the delusion, music held a secret message which left and never came back, instead over many years, without me taking actual notice, through a plethora of books, I read and listened to, and movies I watched pointed to, the SECRET message.

A real bummer. A painful difficulty.

Not every book or movie or television show, held the message, just a unique few. Say fifty or so and I have not read or watched, heard but an ultra-minority of all stories told, spoken, written or made, but I will mention five (movies) with a quickie explanation as a highlight, nothing more.

Five movies:

Matrix–The pills

Inception–Levels of dreams

Good Will Hunting–Faking who I am. My insight, understanding.

A beautiful mind–A false secret message. (I do not see people who are not there) I have other issues.

Glass–I believe against all logic. (I am no super hero, nor do I have multiple personalities)

Short and sweet, but deeply potent, at leased from my point of view. Each of these held power to unseat me, as if, they pointed a hidden finger into the eye of my delusions, my crazy place.

I stood firm, tried not to speak about the squirrelly lessons or deep-seated messages ringing with a beating resonation I believed I found, saw and understood in these stories and so many more. As I said, "I TRIED," but failed, like I have so many other times in my embryonic life. Actually, I spoke my questionable thoughts to numerous people over many seasons, trying to tie together the SECRET MESSAGE. Most of the time my broken insight fell on deaf ears. When it seemed to take a bit of root, good fruit never materialized. A significant part of life, I have come to understand, most human forget, as their minds drift to other, more important areas. They easily overlook weird things as a sure, pure benefit tilted toward my benefit.

My crazy talk remained buried under the surface way under parched and lifeless dirt. Good thing too. Water those seeds and the produce is not pretty. A deception I gave into is the belief, magnificent, incredible, colorful, other dimensional, with miracle working power, life giving fruit would pour forth once I pulled the string. Instead, oozing poisonous mocking destruction flowed, unfiltered as a by-protect. I refuse to call it fruit. Death takes life it never created, had no ownership in the origins, and deserves no recognition except to be cast into oblivion and buried as an ancient forgotten toothless, powerless, frigid, deceiver.

Here is the deal. The lie held a singular purpose. Detach my mind from stability, balance and normality.

The false map.

A super-duper geometrical spectrum with perfect undefinable living grids appeared as a tempting backdrop before my unfocused vision. An invisible map I saw in the secret place of my mind with multiple dimensions leading to the true destination all human beings seek. Fully diagramed, perfectly laid out, connecting all parts at each point to every life form across the never-ending cosmos to the outmost and farthest galaxy, trillions of light years away, and all the way down to the smallest strand of DNA in anyone of multi billions of living obscure individual life forms.

Pick and choose.

Go wide and far or further in than you could ever imagine.

I have heard many individuals, from various diverse religious sects, nationality, genetic origins, educational spectrum, (my way to say, traditionally educated or self-taught) say the phrase, WE ARE A UNIVERSE UNTO OURSELVES, or something of the sort. It doesn't matter. The point is the same. A pure and sure declaration of one of the undeniable truths of life.

Without oxygen, water, light, love and consciousness we do not exist.

WE ARE A UNIVERSE UNTO OURSELVES.

A brilliant observation or a crack pot theory? A deceptive component in my psychosis.

Good thing tools exist to quantify specifics and give the uneducated pictures and a bit of proof.

In case you didn't know the place in this vast expansive universe where, WE ALL EXIST, is in the lower quadrant on the south end of the outskirts, (call it the GHETTO) of a less than a spectacular galaxy, they, who are they? I do not know, but, THEY, call it the MILKY WAY, the point is specific. Creatures who live less than a blink regarding the, what do they call it, billions and billions of years since the BIG BANG, this is a theory, a philosophy, one way to explain the unexplainable. Do not worry, it is only one of many explanations.

Survival of the fittest. Let me say that again. SURVIVAL of the FITTEST. The fit ones survive.

EVOLUTION. A brilliant and powerful scientific theory.

Turning the preverbal coin over there is another view. If you do not come to understand and believe the right way, eternity may be hell.

Some call this religion. Faith. Belief.

A higher power. Give me twelve steps to walk up.

ETERNITY MEANS FOREVER.

How come all of us evolved creatures have not jumped on the bandwagon to accept the seemly better choice. We evolved and, for GOD' sake live by the true-blue law, SURVIVAL of the fittest.

TAKE, TAKE, TAKE.

Blame others seems as a preferred cop out position. Those religious, war monger hold to a message over light and truth.

Those reprobate unbelievers refuse to give GOD the glory and found themselves burned at the stake.

For many billions of years, according to the evolutionists, or thousands of centuries, the true believers state, this battled waged. Written history is imperfect, but I have come to confirm, holds a sizeable amount of stability. A slight jittery place to study, look, observe and discover.

Truth or a big lie.

Cross your fingers.

Be thankful for the historians. Regardless of their spiritual or scientific leanings.

Multitudes have the answer, but none can prove if an enormous bang or an intelligence brought about this inconceivable existence we share for a very short period.

Did God create the HEAVENS and EARTH or did an amazing indescribable, wonderful sophisticated accident happen?

The unprovable question.

The battle.

Intelligent design, or a mystical mix of energy, mass, light, time and space? Or is there no reason at all?

Well, well than. A question worthy to ponder.

Jump on the train, join the club, preach to the rafters. A revelation. The one genuine answer.

So good, containing a bright shining hope to what do you call it, self-awareness, consciousness, creative ability, emotional, self-perceptive existence from an accidental BANG or an intricate well designed, planned graceful act infused by an intimate benefactor.

GOD or Oops?

One or the other. I could not find another possibility. Some twisty turned alterations sure but in the end, creator or nature? We all have to come to grips and deal with simple cards dealt to us and all the voices screaming from places of childish wounds and guilt-ridden condemnation against the sweet, soft, almost silent whisper of echoing, pure resonation of GRACE.

The GOODNESS of GOD and HIS incalculable GRACE, no matter WHAT!!!

No matter what.

Who will hear? Who will come? Why is the message of new life so tainted?

Will the SON of MAN find faith on earth when HE returns?

I used to think so, now I cry with tears too large to hold a thousand oceans.

GOD have MERCY.

I have exposed a bit of my bias. I have believed in GOD my whole life. Not sure why?

Makes me think about Christopher Hitchens. I loved him. I found so much gratification, listening, reading watching him debate all the people who held my same philosophies, beliefs or DARE I say FAITH as mine.

I do not want to spent time going through the internet to make sure I get all the fact right and I may come up short and get some of Mr. Hitchens's words out of contexts, but with my whole heart I am only pouring forth my deep-seated appreciation for his conviction and solid reasoning skills. I still watch him from his early days all the way up until, with his head shaved, I think because of cancer, he fought to defend his well thought out reasoning with persuasive power, his conviction and it makes me shiver.

Christopher Hitchens was a fantastic exceptional human being and I am very sad he does not exist here anymore. A true thinker, an honest soul and one who I completely disagreed with, in the most part.

Disagreement should never equate to HATRED.

He is one of the purest, clearest, unashamed, most well-reasoned ATHIEST I never met, but I spent hours watching and hearing him as an individual. An individual like me, even though he never persuaded me and I am certain I would never have convinced him, nor would I want to. He is, maybe, the greatest apologist for the message of "THERE is no GOD, all this religious shit is a fantasy, causing immeasurable pain and suffering across the globe for centuries, of our age.

Maybe not.

Either way, he is still is a powerful voice, with a wonderful spirit, which is silent now, a real bummer, and I am sad.

Christopher Hitchens, the ultra-atheist, anti-religious zealot still speaks big wisdom in our new time, but HEY, everyone will die, and so did he. One place ALL can agree on without argument including the fact the shells we live in will decay and the worms will eat our brains.

A fantastic circle of life to confound the, SO-CALLED wise.

Throw stones or bow down and repent and find life. Fight and maybe you will live. Argue and maybe in the end, only one statement will survive on the, I guess, a server bay, they call the cloud.

The cloud. Such a great unintended description.

YOUTUBE. Search and you will find.

"Mr. Hitchens, what if you are wrong in your belief when you die?" The big question he always got. HOW SMALL, HOW SAD AND HOW despicable.

Take your pick and choose.

The decision has severe consequences. At least for those of us alive.

Turning to the survival side of the argument, I always wondered who is the fittest.

Going back to evolution.

SURVIVAL of the FITTEST. They teach this as fact in public funded, union paid and monopoly protected schools. It is science, proven fact as a "theory."

Who can ask where the emperors' clothes are and what about the man behind the curtain?

WHO are the fittest? The bullies? Scumbags? Losers? The offenders?

Are victims, you know those abused, ripped off, kicked, beaten, left for dead in the gutter, the fittest?

Call the Department of EDUCATION, (WHO ARE THEY?) and ask a simple question. Who are the fittest?

The humble or the proud. There are differing opinions going back centuries and further.

Beat the crap out of your neighbor and take all his shit, or humble yourself and give and LOVE your neighbor? Who is weak and who is strong? Who is fittest the PUBLIC EDUCATION system has hands down determined in undeniable science?

We all die and rot is indisputable. The rest is up for argument, conviction or faith.

Such a wonderful world.

The crippled, the starving, the poor and those who suffer? The overlooked ones. The humble, the meek, or the ones of a certain race. I guess it is those with big muscles, big guns, strength and power. Those who can MURDER, stomp to death and take charge. The fit ones. Who are the survivalists? Forgive me the "SURVIVAL of the FITTEST."

History has proven those who are fit fall and shift, take place and stand as they take over and abolish.

Over centuries this is an undeniable fact on many continents and through countless regimes.

Call me a liar. I don't mind.

The Pharaohs of Egypt, Nebuchadnezzar of Babylon, Xerxes and Alexander, (they called that piece of shit, "THE GREAT.") OH, MY goodness, what? Are you kidding me?

Alexander, where is he? Dead and gone, his bones are dust.

But let's go back and pull out the fact. Dig deep, look through the archives, pull out the dusty, hand written, parchments over many, many seasons and more times than you can count on your two sets of fingers, brutal, horrifying, incomprehensible. Free for-all genocides. Clear and simple. Caused by the religious and the atheists alike and suffered across the globe.

Red, brown, yellow black, white, original on a continent, or foreign invader, evil, murder, kind, giving, joyful or grief stricken we are a race, THE HUMAN RACE.

Slavery existed as an economical, normal excepted COMMERCE for thousands of years. An unquestioned part of economics.

Disgusting. Abhorrent.

Good thing a new philosophy took hold. At least back then, the slave owners and sellers believed in GOD and, what is it called "Divine Superiority," I could be wrong, but I did not live back then so I cannot say for certain. Truth reigns in both history, science and faith. Does survival of the fittest means this?

Own another human being? Or many others?

Give me a break.

The worms have sucked the brains out, for centuries, THOSE who were the fittest?

I guess the worms win in the end.

I could keep going through the Roman empire, Ottoman, British, the little tiny weeny, Neapolitan, on an on an on an on. A painful, despicable and shameful list could ensue, but I do not want to go down that path. The end is horrifying. Worse than horrifying. In all reality, worse than unbearable.

UNBEARIBLE, UNBEARIBLE, UNBEARIBLE.

Vulgarity is a gutter language.

I understand and in many parts of my being I bend in full agreement to keep my language, my words checked, back in the coat rack, away from women and children. I tend to go out of my way to show honor and respect, hold my tongue, speak with one hand tied behind my back and work with diligence not to offend. Pure people deserve protection. The innocent should not find themselves polluted with the unconscionable grotesque world and the gutter language it creates.

May the sweet and good find protection and supernatural hands over their ears and heavenly blinders over their eyes in this tremulous world.

I am going to ramble a bit, as if I haven't been, but as a side note, I intended to go down a huge, fiery focused certain path, I did not know it would take so long. I have a lot running around through my mind, sorry. I need to make a confession. A sad and emotionally painful confession. My tweaked, out of step and delusional whacked out mind guided my path verbally and with conviction and with utter shame and massive regret I spoke my frustrating nutty thoughts to the first of the seven, more than once.

GOD have mercy.

"Film this diatribe, I have an important message."

Oh, the shame, I literally came to believe I tapped into a brilliant insight and poured it out, gushed and puked it out to the first of the Beautiful Perfect Seven, a horrible incoherent polluted river of words.

Instead of many pages, I am going to spread out a tamed down version as I believe it is still part of my journey to stability and living in a place of balance.

Hold on for a bit and I hope to get back on track.

Remember, PULL the STRING?

A simple detour to relive and shine a light on a terrible rambling screwed up thought pattern. One of many.

Somehow, I thought the light came to me with revelation. This happens almost as a natural seed to water for growth with a harvestable insight. Sometimes it has been an idea I created a business from over many years and financial risk, other times it comes in, as a fully completed, fantastic understanding I lived with in euphoria, until I turned away, let it go, and came to grips with a truth.

Just another whacked out philosophy.

Happened hundreds of times throughout my life.

Here is one.

A bad and humiliating one I wish I could have stuffed back in the bottle of crazy. Instead I poured it out to one of the most beautiful, perfect ones.

Oh, the shame.

I literally called it Vulgarity.

Vulgarity as a message I will take some clicks on the keyboard to wash it out. Otherwise I fear it will dig down and fester, turn into fuel for the crazy to latch onto and blow forth.

Thanks for understanding.

Here it is.

Vulgarity? Words or actions?

I saw a message, THE LIGHT, a one true, specific, SPOKEN WORD, which needed immediate filming to keep for posterity and broadcast across high horizons, across the World Wide Web.

WWW.com

One undeniable fact, being overlooked, remained out in the open, remained with a profound accusing finger to all of society as a blinking corrosive judgmental beam. The dust heap of history waits in the wings to mock the grotesque, evil and suffering inflicted as the absolute most vulgar fact of our race.

This human race.

"RED, BROWN, YELLOW, BLACK and WHITE, they are all precious in his sight. JESUS, loves the little children of the world."

Without mentioning "Idi Amin" of Ugandan or "Pol Pot" of Cambodia, allow me to only bring up three.

Call it millions of MURDERED human BEINGS in Africa and south east ASIA, but HEY, survival of the fittest. Get your second-grade book out AND SING THE SWEET SONG OF EVOLUTION.

Science don't ya know. State funded, free public education.

The killing fields and hacked to death innocent children of GOD have long since left the headline and linger back in the archives. Many decades have come and gone.

The vulgar truth remains.

MILLIONS OF DEAD. Millions and millions and millions. Did I say millions?

If you do not want to read the word "FUCK" cover your years or skip ahead.

I will speak with an open heart, clear mind and beating furious spirit.

Fuck Adolf Hitler!

Fuck him and everyone who followed him and carried out the most horrific debaucheries. FUCK them all.

Pure and simple.

FUCK HIM and his socialist, fascist, utilitarian party with grotesque roots in eugenics.

Some say six million. ARE YOU SERIOUS? Go to a stadium and listen to the crowd cheer for a football game, baseball game or a rock concert. Easy to see, massive amounts of excited people around cheering, getting a HOTDOG, a beer. Seventy of those stadiums full of cheering people does not even touch the surface of the horrific genocide and all the inhuman vulgar butchery. A small percentage. Millions and millions and millions. Jewish families, Catholic's, Roma families, disabled, homosexuals, ethnic minorities and so many others, the counting is a sick worthless effort. IT HAPPENED.

Survival of the fittest.

And what about Mao Zedong of the Communist People's Party of china and uncle Joe Stalin of the old defunct Soviet Union? They made the gas chambers created by the National Socialist party of fascists in Germany look tame.

Fuck them.

Why and how are we able to say "Killed Millions" and not keel over in heart wrenching grief? This is vulgarity not the word FUCK.

I mean what the fuck. How can this be?

At least there are only a few philosophies nowadays. Sure, there are gobs of political, countless religious dogmas, doctrine and waves of human idea, but all in all in reality it comes down to the big two.

Evolution? Creation?

Science is great, but lacking. Faith is great, but unprovable. A dilemma. A quandary and an exciting truth.

WE ARE NOT THE CENTER of the universe, far from it.

A powerful fact. An awesome and magnificent truth. None of us as big dog human beings, nor this wonderful planet in our solar system, nor our place in our galaxy, nor the place our galaxy exist in the universe, are at the center.

Good news.

Gives me an incongruent feeling of hope and comfort.

This galaxy of billions of other planets, stars, with massive violent destruction, incredible energy, mathematical defined laws, pushes and pulls and for some, out of any quantifiable reason, has billions and billions of miniscule specks of life forms, which I HAVE COME TO CONCLUDE, contain a profound value and for some reason are able to speak, learn, argue, disagree, go to war or lay DOWN their existence for others over unconfirmed philosophies and heart felt beliefs, IT MAY BE FAITH OR DECEPTION.

What is that all about?

Even though this obscure, easily overlooked broken boulevard and dead-end galaxy, in this indescribable massive expanse of a universe which to me, seems to be a bastard, stepchild of dying stars contains billions of cognizant, conscious, self-aware individuals who feel, love, kill, fear, feel pain, dream, fight, hope.

I could go on with endless lists of emotions. What is that all about?

The point is, INDIVIDUAL. COGNIZANT. COUNSCIOUS. SELF AWARE.

EVOLVED or DESIGNED?

Take your pick and then fight your guts out. Go to war over your opinion.

OH, the frailty of life.

A unique and powerful question.

Where did I come from? Where am I going?

My first uneducated thought is, LOOK AROUND. As a unique, separate, individual, isolated soul, study, confirm, argue, rest and think, then take time to decide.

Two undeniable truths.

We all die and we all are tiny, less than small compared to the minuscule parts, of outer space with PHOTOGRAPHED evidence, diagramed and studied.

I guess if you are attractive, have fame, a powerful job, a nice butt, big bucks, (THAT MEANS CASH IN THE?) Oh, I don't know in this digital world. They may still call it a bank. How nice. Strut around like a peacock and give some scraps of your bread to the millions of refugees who seek a better life on this big blue and green Orb spinning in the gutter, the alley, ash heap, of the least deserving corner of a galaxy among billions, billions and billions of others.

Strut, be proud, put others down and feel big, or lay yourself down for another.

I get a little preachy at times. Another struggle I need to deal with. Let me try to get back on track.

We are all separate and alone in a pretty fascinating biological shell, but who really cares or thinks about it. No one can do anything about our shared quagmire.

Right?

Pull the String.

This thinking turned a cork screw into my mind, intellect, core, until it squeezed my physical body, and I lost the real clear ability to hold on to sanity, so I gave in with all my heart to float away to arrive at another dimension where I concluded, FANFARE and celebratory victory would burst forth in an imaginary existence I somehow created without knowing.

A beautiful, majestic, fantastic land, world, universe, other place.

THE OTHER PLACE.

Call the white coats who hold the keys to the paddled cells.

But I always felt, THE PLACE, THAT PLACE, the other place, is where I really existed and there are no white coats there, and no padded cells either, so hey, PULL the string and go.

Go to THE OTHER REALM.

Where I really exist.

From my early years, through adolescent, into adulthood, I kept hidden this weird issue for the most part. More times than I can count, I popped my messed-up head above normality and spoke out with incoherent gibberish, but it turns out no one noticed.

A sad truth and on the other hand a real gift.

The string floated just outside my physical perception. I could not see it, but it is green and gold in color.

A green golden string I cannot see.

YIKES.

Hello, this fact alone should have woken me up or snapped me into some place of recognition to the tilt I leaned toward on the balancing scale of reality. Instead I wholeheartedly embraced a mystical, delusional, and by the way, completely, false, illusion which supersedes logic, rational thinking and I, no one else, made a conscious choice to take hold to pull and go.

The flapping temptation outside my view in some sort of magnificent geometrical spectrum with perfect lines making up awesome quadrants, (GRIDS) with living power beseeching me to take hold, pull and take a ride on the one true galactic superhighway so I could or would arrive in the place of my actual, real existence, took over, convinced me and I gave in and PULLED.

Cuckoo.

Welcome to the new world. A celestial existence, beyond sight or sound, body or limitation. An existence in the stars, the one true existence of light and energy.

Side note, there is no real string, the galactic super highway, does not exist, the whole idea is a crock of shit, but I believed it and I did it. I REACHED OUT, PINCHED and PULLED; God forgive me, I did. HOOK LINE and SINKER, whole hearted, fully engaged, all in.

Oh, the shame.

I reached out, caved in, finally, took the risk, maned up and with faith and conviction, pulled and waited to fly away.

What happened you may wonder?

Nothing. Nothing. Nothing, except my mind snapped after it twisted, flipped and flopped and tied itself into dozens of unbreakable knots.

The worst part, the real, huge, insurmountable, enormous, problem, the one I still need to come to grips with, haunts me to no end. I made a conscious choice to leave THE BEAUTIFUL PERFECT SEVEN.

No tears could pour forth from me to wash away this horrible action.

NO TEARS.

As I stand a distance outside the episode, and work to uncover the origins, come to grips and seek help to live in stability and balance, an emotionally painful recognition fills me with sorrow. I made a conscious, although demented choice, to believe the beautiful, the perfect, the magnificent seven did not exist.

MY absolute worst shameful decision.

Crazy is the word and I receive it and am working to come back, humble myself and walk with a stable gate.

A polluted mind, a sick mind, an Ill mind, is no excuse, and holds no power to wash away the deep regret and overwhelming grief at my choice. Tears are a side product, bringing recognition I have real problems.

Thoughts, beliefs, tendencies, perception, intellect, all need to be taken with a pinch of salt from a critical viewpoint, at least in my case. At a moment's notice, out of the blue I could find myself tripped up and spinning out of control.

One way I have dealt with this dilemma, is to be open and transparent with three people I trust who have agreed to let me share some of my crazy before it gets too far out of control. So far so good, but I am in the early stages in a new world with a slight hope to live in stability and balance.

Wow, that section turned out to be very difficult to unfold. Not the humiliation, or ugly reality, the actual mental, emotional battle, brought physical, nauseating fatigue, exhaustion.

Weird.

Glad to move on.

The diagnosis

I have been told we have a pole in us. Makes me think of the north and south poles holding together the enormous crystal blue sphere we exist on floating in the orbital unseen gravitational pull taking us where we have no control over, or an iron stake pounded in the ground to keep dogs from running away. Either way, high and lows, manic and depressive. I get it.

The first go to became, stick your tongue out and swallow this little pill. The pill made in a factory somewhere, from a company you could never find, but trust us, swallow and all your dreams will come true, or nightmares may ensue and take over, but do not worry we will meet with you and take notes.

Fantastic.

Manic Depressive Disorder, "Bipolar" with some Psychosis is the diagnosis. I have a short pole, with significate swings. High and low. Sometimes I feel sideways. I don't think there is a medication for going sideways. Oh wait, let's not go there.

Crap.

I have also been told I am depressed, with a possible biochemical imbalance. As a biological creature, this makes sense. Out of balance. Oddly enough I seem to connect and resonate with the issue of biochemical imbalance the most. Might be this is a place I feel able to quantify and have some control over.

I swung on the pole. Mostly on the manic side, always have, but I accept and agree with the swings. Depression as a diagnosis does not speak a whisper of truth though. Although it seems logical, I went through depression and this is not that, thank God. Flowing tears feels like a gift compared to sleeping all the time to escape torment.

There are specific, although with a bit of ambiguous flexibility, treatment options.

Medications.

They might think about changing the name to medicine. Treating sickness, mind sickness or illness in this case with medication leaves the idea of rolling the dice. Put your money down and see if black or red come up. Medicine seems to be a cure, or at least an effective treatment. Headache, give me some medication? No, I need an Aspirin, Tylenol, Ibuprofen.

Where is the Medicine?

For the mind, there are medications. "Anti and Stabilizing" medications. Antidepressants, Antianxiety, Antipsychotics and mood stabilizers. Three "anti" to one "stabilizing". Guess the anti holds the cards in this fight. The milligrams vary wide and far. The names and companies differ as well. The patent holders, these are the owners who took the risk and created the drug call, NAMEBRAND, and the copy cats, GENERIC.

Lots and lots and lots. Numerous options all with small print detailing, what do they call them?

SIDE EFFECTS.

Enter at your own risk.

I have some of these drugs in my drawer and can pop the lid at any time. I have chosen to hold off for a season at this point and I get it, the internet if full of one explicit statement.

"If they stop taking their medications bad things happen."

It seems to be the perfect banner ad for bipolar treatment:

"YOU HAVE TO STAY ON YOUR MEDS, or else?"

Nanny, Nanny, Nanny goat.

Here is a creepy delusion or a fascinating horror story, either way, I literally thought and played with an intricate, diabolical, messed up fear-based conspiracy theory in my mind, for several days until I had all the components for a first draft of a terrifying novella. Imagine, I actually did cave in with a gusto, the medications which will make all my answers to the questions come true.

"How are you doing?" with only one just one, response.

"GREAT. I am doing wonderful. These medications have perfect miracle working power. I WILL NEVER STOP TAKING THEM. Thank you for helping me."

Music to the ears of the pill pushers. What could be better than getting paid to listen each week for an hour and chalk up success to their brilliant treatment? Do a seminar, boast and give a humble smile to the pats on the back.

But what if the meds, MEDICATIONS, caused the ginny pig, the crazy lab rat who faithfully swallowed on time and a daily basis, became trapped behind the wall of their mind with tormenting voices pounding relentless evil, vitriol, terror, deception, temptation day and night, until the rug gets ripped out to the crescendo of laughing, mocking howls.

"YOU WILL LIVE UNDER THIS torment FOR THE REST OF YOUR life. You can only state when asked how you are doing with a creepy reply of GREAT, the meds are a miracle." HEE, HEE, we got you now. Our prisoner who can tell no one and you cannot kill yourself. HEE, HEE.

Here is a real-life experience.

Not a horror story, although looking back several components attach in my memory send chills through my bones, and shine with a sharp blade into my reality. A sign post. Part of my life I left behind years ago and now find myself going back to with the best intent, unsure of the outcome. I already recognize some blaring specifics, personal judgments, protective measures I used to side step the sharply focused threat.

Remember my excuse? "I was just a kid." I am no longer a child so here we go.

Like a light switch flicking off, my mother snapped, and turned off. She went from beaming laughter, joy, hope, into a zombie like depression, on a dime. For the first eight years of my life she did not have any outward symptoms, in fact she held a solid, powerful strength of stability and capability. Somewhere around my eighth birthday or during that year, the wheels came off the train, literally. Snap, from normality to a dark, web covered, lifeless dungeon. All light and life left my mother's eyes, and it never returned all the way until she died.

This is an issue.

As a kid, I didn't really care and did not worry or consider. I lived on a selfish pogo stick, bouncing around like a buzzing bee. My peripheral vision went less than two degrees from my own desires. I lived fast, small, without concern, with my whole mind focused on ME.

Baseball, soccer, riding bikes, skateboarding and the greatest of all, GIRLS. They were everywhere back then, and I noticed all of them, and went out of my way to talk with them. I was no predator or fiend, only a giddy boy who liked every single one and I could talk. Like an auctioneer.

Life was better than good.

Not for my mother. A darkness over took her outside of my notice. Looking back, I remember the times she went to the mental hospital. Not sure they call it that anymore. I believe impatient or a lock down facility now is the name. Either way, I visited her with others in my family. Weirdly enough I do not remember ever talking with my siblings about this issue until many years later.

I remember my father saying, "when mom gets out it will take a long time until she gets better," whatever that meant. As far as I remember she never did and we moved over and over hoping it would do the trick. There is no trick and here I am looking to my own issues for longevity, stability and balance. This is one reason I am taking time and not looking for the quick fix. Tears, anxiety, weird thoughts will not kill me and I have no thought or interest in hurting myself or anyone else. PERIOD. I have three who I trust and have agreed to be wide open before, and I have agreed and have given them balanced authority to work with each other for my benefit. So far so good.

Prejudice.

Pre-judgment is a very clear part of my mindset when it comes to anti or stabilizing mind medication-based treatment. I am not exaggerating. Numerous pill bottles lined the window sill in our kitchen for years. I never knew what was in the bottles, I only remember the sound and time it took to open each one and the shaky swallow that ensued.

Not all, but many days I went through a ritual. My mother dressed in slippers and a bathrobe shuffled into the kitchen, hair muffed, hands trembling with shaky twitters, falling into a chair, head down cast, working on the limited strength she had to take on the task of injection and then going for the pill bottles.

An early life onset of diabetes required a daily injection of insulin my mother needed to take. I guess for most of her life. I never gave much thought to it, even though for some odd reason she gave herself the injections in the kitchen each morning. Just part of life. When she fell into one of her downward stupors, giving herself the injection of insulin would be a nearly insurmountable task, So I assisted. I gave her the shot.

Fresh syringe, certain milligrams or whatever they call it, from the insulin bottle, stick the needle in her thigh, push down, place the cap over the needle of the syringe and throw it in the trash. Quick, simple, maybe it took forty seconds, no big deal. Then came the pills. Ten to fifteen minutes of hell ensued, I still cringe thinking about the daily ordeal.

Nowadays they have the Sunday, through Saturday, plastic pill holders. What a brilliant invention. Not back then, or if they did, not in our house. Each bottle needed an investigative study, talked about, argued over, with the purpose explained in excruciating detail, with a cup of water needing to be filled twice as pill after pill went down the pipe. Not all were mind meds. Some were to counter the side effect from the drugs. "This causes constipation so I need the stool softener," things like that. As many pills for the side effects as the cure of illness of the mind, maybe more.

Disgusting.

The worst is when there would be a new fancy DANCY, drug to try. Throw out the old and bring in the new. So eager, so hopeful, but my mother never came back. In fact, she lived a sad life as a walking drug infused zombie for all my adult life and each and every birth of the perfect seven.

So sad and pitiful.

At one point my mother found a diagnosis of "Parkinson's disorder." This is not Parkinson's disease, it is a disorder, mimicking the disease stemming from an over load of toxins from decades of chemical treatment for mental illness. The pills caused the disorder. How horrible, how despicable, how down right evil.

Physical attributes of Parkinson's disease caused by an over load of factory created chemicals to treat sadness.

MENTAL ILLNESS.

WHAT the FUCK?

Oops, vulgarity.

How vulgar are the BIG pill pushers, the BIG payors and the BIG government who keep this despicable system running?

I hear the tune from Jeopardy ringing in my ear.

The answer is SELF EVIDENT.

I guess you can see some of my concerns, a small sliver of my struggle and maybe a slight gander into my confusion over which one of the multitudes of medications I should take. Well then, take your pick, hold your nose, put your finger to the breeze, lick it and choose. One, two or three. The blue one, the red one? You cannot say and either can I. The debt infused, degree holding, ignorant of how taxes work, or how compounded interest accrues, are peddling this shit. In the old days we would have sent them to jail for SELLING DRUGS. Today they hand the drugs across the counter with SUPER DUPER rich, BIG, third-party payors taking up the tab for only a small co-pay.

What the???

Oh gosh, GOLLY?

WHAT is VULGARITY?

Give me a break.

The pill pushers my mother listened to and followed like a junk yard dog are surly dead by now. An unhealthy struggle I contemplate turns to the simplistic. Did any of those ineffective head shrinks know the names of her children, her favorite color or the city my mother grew up in?

Shame on them and the scripts they scribbled out. Drug pushers who never went to jail.

Drugs the GOVERNMENT sanctioned as prescriptions.

The SCRIPTS.

Looking back, a true, out of the norm option opened up and became a genuine possibility. A short-lived possibility. It came from my older siblings. As one of the younger ones I went along without too much input. I remember one of my brothers, he is dead now, asking my mom to do a few bong hits, only to see if it helped. Just a hit off a pipe, no cocaine, heroin, hash, Quaaludes, LSD, only try the weed and see if it does any good.

It did not go over well although my brother gave some of the best persuasive words which could have pierce the armor of decades of the fortresses built on unmovable rocks of generational philosophies set in stone. I still admire the effort, but it did not have any impact. In the end the only treatment came from the writers of the scripts.

I have no temptation to smoke or snort illegal substances nor do I have an intent, TODAY anyway, to follow the path of mode stabilizers or anti-anxiety meds, but I appreciated my long since dead brother's heart felt interest in seeing our mother helped in any way possible.

Most days I do not feel any need to look for a fix, but at times, which can come out of nowhere as the rubber meets the road, I find myself tempted to cave in and say yes to the persuasive tempters. The pushers.

Either take seven hits of acid, or give in and say yes to the PROFESSIONAL pill pushing chemical prescribers.

Suck down their assumptive options. See if they work.

There are concerns.

Let's be clear the quasi professionals have not done a good job. Their profession has a dismal history of less than pristine results and they have no ability to follow up to quantify their value. It seems to me, no investigative reporter has taken the time to get to the bottom of this muddy quagmire, but the facts appear to prove this system, these head shrink's, the sophisticated and knowledgeable, highly decorated and degree stricken have led multitudes of mentally disabled LAMBS to the slaughter.

Where are the bleeding hearts to publish a story? Expose the facts?

I guess I made myself heard about my thoughts when it comes to phycological based prescription driven legal medication treatment. I could go back over it and reiterate and I could do it over and over, which is a weird tendency I have. To REPEAT things.

In case you haven't noticed.

Oh well.

The next path of treatment is called Psychotherapy.

A terrible name at least from where my mind twists and spins. Therapy seems as the accepted word these days, as this part of treatment.

Talk Therapy.

Weekly in most cases for an hour or so. Rant and rave or share deep-seated emotions out loud to a highly trained professional. I believe this type of treatment holds slight favorable components.

First, there is hope in getting out your thoughts, experiences, background, worries, fears, and dreams which gives anticipation in advance of the meeting. There is a value in anticipation, it produces a place for possibility, maybe a breakthrough, but in the end, it does not achieve the anticipated results. No fault or blame is placed on the form or those in need, only a non-predetermined, but factual observation.

Weekly in ineffective.

Second, I have come to see a legitimate need to speak to other human beings is very important. Friends, family, acquaintances, strangers, and let's call them professionals. Hard to quantify why this need exists, and I have heard several, well thought out reasons. I believe it is part of the human make-up, how we were created. The important need for connection and also to be heard and understood.

Talking about issues can also make things worse. When you go down to the internal place there is the opportunity to stay there. Weekly talking does not always pull you out and can leave an unfulfilled place of incomplete release, so it is important to have wisdom on what and how much you spill out. I am only saying this from my individual and limited experience.

Historical background, personal relationships, disappointments, excitements, likes and dislikes are perfect for an hour setting. Crazy talk needs to be prepared in advance and limited to the scheduled amount of time so a resolution has the possibility to materialize otherwise, a creepy unease lingers for an extended period.

This also comes from my experience.

One of the primary purposes I have chosen to tap, hunt and peck this out as personal written talk therapy is, I have not found a single person I could dump all this out on nor would it be appropriate. So, I have chosen YOU! Thanks for listening. Writing this has proven to be beneficial. You should have seen some first rambles I puked on paper. My oh my. I cut pages and pages and pasted those to a hidden place. It helps me to go back and read over and it seems appropriate to admit some of what I did not cut can ramble in the direction of the unhealthy, but hey, I am on a journey. I also have three others I trust and talk with weekly, some times more, to round out my treatment plan, keep me accountable and as a confessional and sounding board.

One is a therapist with a PHD, one is a family member and the other is a Spirit filled friend.

Besides talk therapy there are some other parts of mental health I am working to implement I found as value from across the internet which let me tell YOU, there are many thoughts on treatment. I have chosen to focus on three others.

Physical, Mental and Spiritual.

I am in the early stages so I am by no means even in the driver seat moving toward a destination so I feel it would be inappropriate to speak too much here.

Physical.

Sleep, eating right and exercise.

I take naps and work to make sure I at least calculate and follow a regimented sleep pattern. It does not always work, but I have not gone without sleep for more than a day for some time. It is a hit and miss and odd in comparison to the great wide world out there. I am up in the dark most nights, but I go back and rest, fall into a sleep and also, at odd times in the day, I will sleep for an hour or more. Sometimes several times throughout a day. The point is I am sleeping more.

Eating better.

I quit, coffee, alcohol, most food with processed sugar and I simply eat slower with less of an intake. In other words, I do not pound down large portions. Besides the sugar, coffee and alcohol, I do not feel a need for prohibition. So much great choices out there and I partake, only in lower doses and I take time to enjoy the wonder of taste by appreciating each bite. Most of my life my mind raced so fast I never took time to enjoy food. Sure, I had wonderful meals, by my mind remained elsewhere. Now I eat with gratitude and not as a glutton.

Exercise.

I am trying and believe I will find a sweet spot. Getting my heart moving by making my body exercise I believe down deep, holds a value, but do not like the process. I look forward to a day when I feel excited to work out or strengthen my body. Until then, I grudgingly force myself to move.

The big part for me at this point is to get my guts out by writing and trust by the end I will lay out a complete treatment plan for longevity and stability and live a life in balance.

A high calling.

I have a disobedient streak in me so I hope to be faithful to my decision, as I would be going against myself.

I will continue to use my two index fingers to type this out, although I do not know where I am going. It is alright as I lived most of my life on a wild rollercoaster so no big deal here. Until I come to a place where I study medicine or "medication," I will endeavor to share my thoughts, struggles, history as my medicine. I did not self-diagnosis, but I will not bend over, touch my toes and take anything until I can quantify the value and the risks. One day I might, but not in the early stages when those who are pitching pills do not know me or the Beautiful Perfect Seven. I understand when you come in and speak our whack- a- doddle words anyone, trained or novices would pitch and peddle the meds, no problem, but as the one, the recipient, I need some time to quantify the effectiveness, the value, the cons as well as the pros.

My thoughts explode with tormenting fire and then dig down to the deepest part of my being. I lived on a rollercoaster straight up. Now it is extreme shifts. When going up I blast off into the stratosphere, burst open with brilliant beautiful light in every direction, and then the fall feels like a bunker busting bomb exploding with silent darkness across the depths of my whole being. A benefit is neither last too long. In other words, highs are high as low is low, but quick. For my entire life I wanted to scream, open my heart wide, but I lacked the ability until now. I got caught. I am unable to hide any longer. Something broke and I cannot cover up or hide the way I did. How painful, but somehow may prove valuable. As I continue, my goal is to unload with coherency, clarity, leaving aside most rambling or crazy talk, disjointed pivots, quick turns in alignment to my secret internal traveling bone. I will do my best. On the other hand, I have a tendency to wail, moan or scream out loud with babbling incoherent gibberish, but new technology allows deletes, back spaces and I can walk away.

I realize, back in my very early days, I found myself looked down on by a large swath of the world. Interesting enough it seemed to be those who colored inside the lines, followed the rules and did well in school. Those who did not put me down or look down on me seemed to not color inside the lines of life either. An interesting fact. Very telling. Who should we follow, the finger pointers or the acceptors? Just a question. I do not remember one time ever passing a test or a class with anything higher than a "C." I could not sit still or focus to pass the test so I became an outsider.

A dummy.

On the other hand, I knew early on I did not contain a nature of cruelty which I take no credit for, but I am grateful. My

149

problem bents to the other end of the spectrum. I feel such sadness for those who are mean, hurtful, vicious, uncaring. Don't get me wrong, those who offend the innocent, the weaker, are disgusting pieces of shit. No question. But I hold hidden in me a weird compassion and empathy for the disgusting pieces of shit. I have considered, but am unable to quantify the rhyme or any reason, so I move on like I have all my life.

Most of my early life I heard words of accusation against me. Simple words, unambiguous words no one could deny. "Are you stupid? What is wrong with you? How come you can't be like everyone else?" To name a few of the dozen or so accusations.

This incongruency in me illustrates one of hundreds, if not thousands, of painful inconsistency my mind explodes under. On countless occasions I pulled back the curtain of my secrecy, to state clear as day my thoughts and struggles, but out of grace or curse, very few could hear. I put no blame on anyone, in fact it adds icing on the cake of my torment. I would say in my mind, *how could you not hear what I just said?*

Let me give you two incongruent issues as a spark on the fuse threatening to blow my head off. Strap in, buckle up and prepare for takeoff, hopefully with and open mind and blindless ears.

Incongruency.

The United States of America.

In my own conscience I cannot pledge allegiance to a cloth. Red, white and blue, stars and stripes, but I would never let the flag touch the ground or desecrate it in any way. The symbol may be the most powerful expression of incredible goodness and hope, but over a couple hundred years, horrifying injustice and oceans of blood are stitched into the fabric. Thousands and thousands of mostly young, mostly male, brave heroic patriots have given the greatest of all sacrifice. Their own lives. For that alone, I should shut up. I did not serve, what right do I have to say anything? The reason I will continue is for the beautiful perfect seven. The first, second, third, fourth, fifth, sixth and the seventh.

The Seven.

The pledge is to the flag of the United States of America and to the republic for which it stands. I understand it seems like such a small issue. No matter small or big, I cannot pledge my allegiance to a symbol, a piece of cloth, no matter how awesome it might be. You speak this out in the wrong company and watch out, the national guard may be called up and the firing squad set in place. I understand and have for most of my life limited conversations on questionable or provocative issues can and usually do, cause and produce unfruitful endless emotionally driven arguments seasoned in frustration and offense. For those reasons, I have tended to avoid saying my thoughts and if I only contained ten or twelve of these, the effort would have been manageable, but I burst with more than I can count.

I believe the United States of America is the greatest country on earth. Hands down. Period. With seven articles written by a quill pen in candle light a new government came into existence. Plus, the authors, fathers, thinkers, whatever they were, does not really matter they are all dead now, somehow out of brilliant wisdom amended their articles with ten defined areas of restriction against the power of their new government they created. This government shall not, cannot, will not. Some call these the bill of rights other the ten amendments. Either way the constitution and amendments are only a few pages long. Words on a paper, but so powerful and great, except one of the most clearly defined elements is forged in hypocrisy. Freedom. At the time of the formation of the United States government, wooden ships blown by wind over vast oceans to a faraway continent hunted down countless human beings, chained them up, crammed them in and brought them to the greatest nation on earth for one reason.

Fucking profit.

Land of the free home of the brave to live as property to the highest bidder. Slavery not freedom. The grotesque government sanctioned business of slavery is so disgusting and massively incongruent with the founding documents.

"We hold these truths to be self-evident, that ALL men are created equal, that they are endowed by their Creator with certain unalienable Rights, that among these are Life, Liberty and the pursuit of Happiness."

Slavery for profit at the same time annihilation of the separate, district indigenousness peoples from coast to coast, mountains to plains for what? Dirt, rivers and trees. Slavery for profit and annihilation for land and I still believe this is the greatest nation on earth. So much suffering, bloodshed, generations destroyed or wipe out. If I could believe in survival of the fittest this would not be incongruent at all, but I believe in a benevolent creator so I war inside myself.

The Gospel.

I have believed in God since my very first memory. I am not sure why; I only know I did. I naturally prayed and talked with the creator of my soul as a close friend. I went to a catholic mass weekly and catechism monthly. I heard, but did not understand the message of Jesus Christ although I talked to him in my mind and heart. The greatest story of all time or the sure account told by witnesses, the gospel grabbed a hold of me and may be the most incongruent part of life. Everything created by Him for Him and through Him, and He came to this realm as an innocent sacrificial lamb. A blood sacrifice. The creator brutely suffered, nailed to timbers of wood died for all who believe. Stealing the power of death and the grave. A gift to live in eternity where tears pain and sorrow no longer exist. I believe this unbelievable message with every fiber of my being, right down to the smallest stands of my DNA. Whole heartily, unashamed, with an unexplainable powerful confidence. But I also completely understand why others don't believe. What I have difficulty understanding is how those who believe like I do, walk with brash pride and undeniable selfishness. As a true hypocrite I guess. God have mercy. Then on the other hand many who do not believe walk in humility and compassion, serve, sacrifice and give. If God opposes the proud but gives grace to the humble what can be said. Is pure and undefiled religion shown by deeds or by words. Actions or philosophical thought?

One resonator of my long-lost past, told me decades ago, "the words are more important than the miracles."

It took me years to understand and I still struggle.

Give your shirt also if they take your coat. The weak are the strong ones. The greatest serve others. The last are first. So many others in similar upside down and inside out, declarations, teachings all called commands. COMMANDMENTS in a new covenant under GRACE.

The biggest one seems to be, "the work of God is this, believe in the ONE He sent."

Another big one is, "Love your Enemy."

Some of the greatest works of good have come from this gospel. Charitable organizations, hospitals, food kitchens, housing on and on, but so much evil, debauchery and death have come as well. The crusades, the inquisitions, wars, burning people at the stake, in boiling oil, all in the name of the GREAT GOD and SAVIOR JESUS CHRIST.

These are two of the strongest back and forth, contradictory, polar opposites all tied together in my thoughts. The United States government and the Gospel of Grace. There are a variety of many others that seem to hit me out of nowhere. I will hold those for another day, but I am certain some with will seep out.

A powerful stabilizing force came as an unexplainable, but undeniable and underserved gift. Seven gifts in fact. How outstanding, how incredible. Simply outstanding. From a microscopic unsustainable particle of life inside me, grew and formed and delivered into my hands the Beautiful Perfect Seven. Spend too much time on this truth and watch out your mind might detach.

I hid who I am, protected myself from the millions of racing throughs, incongruencies pulsing thorough my heart, igniting billons of connecting points of fire across my whole body. I am deeply sorry. Although I used self-denial as a potent medication, I realize now I denied myself in selfishness and self-protection. I am embarrassed by the crazy in me and I worked hard to lock it up, but now the chains have shattered and I find myself in an uncharted strange land. As a weak broken unprepared and uneducated frail but good intentioned man, I kept my real self hidden. I walked with a lame leg and a blind eye and the seven came as a gift to me anyway. So wonderful with a love so great, so deep it feels unbearable at times.

Although I hold no ability over life, suffering, death or disease, I can work to uncover and bring to light the areas of my life, either by passive choice or overt protection, the unstable actions and cover-ups I allowed to guide my steps.

My goal is to shine a light on the hidden parts I kept locked away in icy darkness with some hope to keep from spiraling into another unseen cesspool of destructive behavior.

I need to start with the pollution.

I polluted myself four specific times in my life and have a tendency to continue. With time for reflection I have a bent toward the compulsive, with an unknown purpose to keep from having to look at the unstable ways the cylinders of my mind fired. I become a master at keeping my mind flying high, with the help of outside influence.

Drugs and Alcohol.

I first smoke pot in the sixth grade. Within a year I smoked weed eight or nine times a day. In addition, I snorted and freebased cocaine, did meth, took numerous hits of acid, ate hallucinogenic mushrooms and got drunk at least weekly. I need to point out I was no island to myself back then. Nearly everyone in the neighborhood engaged. No exaggeration, hundreds of kids all getting wasted. Interesting, most did well in school which I could never achieve for the life of me, but everyone was getting high and they all shared freely. Without giving too much detail, I will state clearly, I continued this abhorrent behavior, daily, until my ninetieth year.

There is some evidence this type of daily chemical over load, in adolescence, can be a cause for several mental illness issues. I can appreciate the well thought out reasoning, but there is no factual evidence and no treatment from the revelation. Washing the toxins out of the brain and pores of the body seems to make some logical sense, although there is no such treatment. Adding new toxins of chemical treatment leaves me scratching my head with a double take. I have concluded the philosophy of an overload of illegal drug use, is very unhealthy and may be a cause of abnormal behavior. Without a mechanism to prove the premise, I reason there is no value for the patient and the professional. It might be a simple excuse for the crazy birds and a plausible reason for abnormal behavior to give slight comfort to the therapist. Either way it matters not. I have no excuse. I polluted myself with a massive intake of a wide variety of drugs and gallons of all types of alcohol.

The one step program.

Out of nowhere I went through a life change which has remained with me to this day. It came by way of hitching a ride. This is when you stick your thumb out on the side of the road and a stranger pulls over and gives you a ride, free of charge, no questions asked. Anyway, this forty something man, who it happens I worked with, pulled over, picked me up and drove me home. On the way, he held up a book and asked, "do you know what this is?" I said, "the Bible." He responded, "God's road map for life," and proceeded to explain a simple and clear message of the Gospel. The main point, "None of are good, all have sinned, the lamb of God came and went through a horrible bloody death, rose again and whoever believes in Him, the blood sacrifice wipes out everything and makes you fresh and clean so we can live forever without, pain, sorrow or tears.

GOOD NEWS. Great news.

In one single day, BING, no more drugs, no more alcohol, cigarettes, pornography, masturbation, in a single day. All gone. Night and day. Washed or transformed, released, freed, I do not have the exact word, all I know is one day I lived one way, the next a completely different way all based on a simple message I believed. Not by my effort, ability, gritting my teeth. Hard to explain other than a clear undeserving miracle.

I shined with a wide smile and wanted to tell everyone one I knew. It did not go well. A bit discouraging when people you know, care for, love, feel judged, because of zealous excitement over a simple clear message of mercy and grace.

Weird and disconcerting.

GOD LOVES YOU, is somehow a negative statement.

I still struggle over this weird incongruency, but who am I?

I became a dedicated follower and gave my whole heart to this wonderful Savior and beautiful message. Then out of the blue, I found myself pounded from every internal corner of existence. A mind battle. Arguments, literal verbal fights ensued over every conceivable angle. The first one hit me when I read a bible verse, and I heard a sinister accusation in my head. "See, JESUS is the son of God, not God."

BAM, I flung to a passage in the first chapter of Saint John, "In the beginning was the Word and the Word was with God and the Word was God." Then further down in the chapter, "the Word became flesh and dwelt among us."

Gotcha.

I battled like this quite often. Not only regarding scripture but in vast and wide, weird and despicable places. War in the mind. Not good.

I memorized a number specific battling verses. I will highlight them here.

Take every thought captive.

Think on these things which are pure, undefiled.

Set your mind on things above.

Take up a shield to extinguish the flaming missiles of the evil one.

Then I found myself worn out and a crippling horrifying depression took over. I would have four seconds of peace when I woke up and then, WHAM, turned to knots, crumpled and crimped internally. I wondered how many people struggle with this.

A bad thought.

I could not get free for the life of me. I did not consider suicide. I only wanted to feel normal and at peace.

Interesting enough, I found myself accepted to a summer missions' trip to Ecuador. Although completely depressed and sleeping from late afternoon to early morning, I continued to work five days a week. The supervisor over my department gave me a bunch of furniture to sell on my driveway as support for my time in South America. I put all the items out to sell and sat in terrible depression, fatigued desiring to hop in bed for the rest of the day and through the night.

Peace. Rest.

I held firm and thought a deep-seated desire. Could have been a prayer, I cannot fully recall. It went something like this.

"If the plane to Ecuador goes down, I would be happy."

No thought of others on board and their demise. Horrible, but true, I hoped for the plane to crash. A powerful elusive unhealthy desire. A disgusting fantasy.

Severe depression moves far beyond reason.

With the exciting visions of dying in a blazing fire, as a gift, from a crashing airline dancing in my head, a kid rode up on an old stingray bike to gander over some crap set out for sale to help fund my, "MISSION's TRIP." He bought nothing. Hard to remember his age, or any other attributes. Only the unforgettable physical, spiritual and mental battle unleashed.

Hell peeked its grotesque head from behind the curtain of oppression and a war ensued.

As I watched the kid move his bike around the items with a hope to find something he might value, I thought about how I longed to go back to the days of bike riding and being excited when I heard the music from the ice cream truck. Beside nostalgia, some compassion rose in me.

There is no way to remember the exact words, and it is unnecessary, the heart, the revelation and hellish battle, the physical release, rings with a powerful clarity.

The kid rode off, and I opened up a prayer inside my head, from my heart. "God, I pray for this boy, protect him, keep him from sorrow or grief and reveal your grace and love to him."

"What, so he can become like you?" I heard as if verbally.

A fire burned in me and I yelled, "I rebuke you devil in JESUS name. Get behind me Satan."

SMACK, ZING, ZIP, the depression evaporated in a moment, and then like an evil thief, right back with crushing power. Crap. "Get out of here devil," again gone, I stood free and normal for less than ten seconds.

Back and forth I yelled in my mind and I think verbally. As I scrambled to put the items back in my garage, this hop, skip and jump, ordeal, like a mental hop scotch and back and forth lethal spiritual volley became a physical battle with evil for at least an hour. I clicked off and screamed my rebukes, with peace and normality infused back in my guts for a few seconds and then the gripping depression grabbed again. Back and forth, back and forth, again and again. Puddles of sweat soaked my hair, face, clothes. It felt like my shoes were filling with lakes of toxins from this internal spiritual war. Because I slept so much, for so long, fatigue and physical weakness could have been the title of my resume. I did not care. I fought with all I had and for ten to fifteen seconds, real peace came in, then WHACK.

HEE, HEE, HEE,

Clicking sharp nails of evil scrapped against the chalkboard of my weak resolve and taunted me.

Not good.

I yelled, "you evil viol disgusting spirit leave NOW!"

I got to a place of about thirty seconds of peace, then forty-five, and a minute.

Deliverance.

No.

I have come to see; memory of depression holds a significant power. When it holds you so tightly, for so long, it is very difficult to forget the darkness and remember what the light of normality feels like.

There is no redeeming value in depression. It sucks life, tares down, steals, kills. Depression is an unrepented enemy and the clearest definition of evil. That is how I see it and that is how I TREATED the familiar foe on the fateful day of the beginning of deliverance in the form of a latter to climb out of the pit of despair.

I would like to say this crippling depression left me by the end of that breakthrough day. It took weeks in stages, and months after to find a complete release to stand firm at the door with tricky knocks to trip me up, open up, and get in to rule the roost leaving me as wiped out road kill.

I was soaking wet, a complete physical mess, fighting like a wounded, dying solider, longing to climb into bed and sleep for a week, but I held firm and left for an evening service at my church. The whole way I screamed, felt normal and then, BINGO.

"I'M BACK, and I will never leave."

Eerie, worse than horrible.

The fatigue became overwhelming, and I almost turned around in defeat. The verbal rebukes were becoming less effective. I almost caved. Then a sweet spark of remembrance whispered a peaceful song into my heart. A simple, although powerful scripture. "We do not war against flesh and blood, but against principalities of the air."

Peace came but only for a moment. Then another whisper. *The principalities of the air were made a spectacle when Jesus Christ rose again from the dead.* This means mocked. This force, this evil, this depression, these voices had been mocked by the resurrection of the Lamb of God. The forces waged against me were ridiculed and defeated.

Peace came, but not for long. I would like to say different, but I realized the answer remained wider and deeper, than screaming my head off every few minutes for the rest of my life. So, I used my tongue, backed by an open broken heart, to make clear melodic declarations. I started to sing. This did not elevate the threat or diminish the torment fully; but it became a powerful addition as a sharp weapon of arrows in my quiver.

I sang, soft and with sincerity. Here are the first verses from three.

"I sing a simple song of love, to my savior, to my JESUS, I am grateful for the things you done."

"I am yours; you are mine, I'm your cup, pour out your wine."

"Amazing grace, how sweet the sound."

Since then, now, many decades later, here is one of my go to songs. It has helped me in times of warfare and struggle, but unfolds some proper questions.

"Great and marvelous are your works, LORD GOD ALMIGHTY. Just and true are your ways oh Lord, you are the king of saints."

Over a long and painful period, I found both my feet, for the most part, on solid ground and able to move in a forward position. Not a straightforward path and it did not come absent of brutal falls and difficult struggles. In fact, during my time in Ecuador, a real world ruthless almost debilitating time came in with a sinister foreign threat. I guess there are regional, forces of evil to sweep us human beings into the ditch, no matter where you find yourself.

Good thing, my job, on "THE MISSION FIELD," held one main purpose.

Pick teams of AMERICAN's, this means from the United States, up from the Airport, take them to the hotel, pick them up and bring them to a job site, this is construction of a church or bible school, while they work all day, I drove around like a chicken with my head cut off, not speaking an inch of Spanish, and picked up boards, cement, roofing material and dropped them off, until the work day ended and I took the teams back for showers and clean-up, while the bright white, hundred and ten pound wife, of the missionary, located and set-up a place for dinner and then back to the hotel for the night.

That turned out to be one massive run-on sentence and I don't even understand grammar and the RULES of the language.

Just saying.

Anyhow, one truth proved to be an asset as I punched and weaved, ducked and jabbed the enemy I knew. The problem seems to appear to be a geographical cabal who need no translation of language. They speak the same universal language. LIES and DECEPTION. When they speak their native language, they LIE. What the Hell? Are you kidding me? This seems to be an unfair advantage. But we, as biological and spiritual beings, hold weapons these reprobates are deaf and dumb too. Unable to hear and do not see coming. A sweet defense and power, against onslaughts and deception, both north and south of the border, although these slimy, squirmy, false speaking reptiles seem to have fairly effective recruitment measures in place.

Amongst others weapons, keeping busy holds a fantastic power. I have used this as one of my most potent arrows ever since. It did not work like a charm, all the time, but I worked with diligence to perfect, sharpen, hone and refine the power and live for decades, proud and boastful with this favorite weapon. Live as an out of control, MANIC, hyper, although soft spoken most of the time, diligent, self-sacrificing, deceiver, all to keep from being taken out.

God please help me.

Those days are over and here I am, naked and wanting, panting and at times frustrated, filled with physical anxiety and downright humiliated.

Beside the hyper schedule I lived with the teams who came to South America to build, "DO MISSIONs" work, there turned out to be one day of relaxation. Saturday, after the week of nonstop work schedule, shopping became the pleasant part of the agenda.

Each team had a day off out of the seven, and my job, on the VACATION day, tilted to going to the market. Showing these out of towner's, the ultra-cheap, hand crafted leather goods, knickknacks or hand carved pieces of art for purchase at a pittance to remember the wonders of South America when they returned to the good old land of the U.S.A. The next day I dropped the group at the airport for departure and picked up a new group from another American city and did it all again. A summer of back-to-back groups and keeping busy.

When I made it back to the States, the aftermath and most of the flash backs, with threats of disabling depression stood outside only an arm's length away, I got busy. My first line of offense, turned out to be religious frenzy. This brought a two-pronged benefit. Keeping super busy through works of service, plenty to do out there, an endless supply. The other place I poured myself into is study, reading, learning, listening, attending.

I went to church at least four times a week and stayed after for hours, talking, going out to eat with a group of others or doing something needing assistance around the place. I listened to Christian radio. Not music, talk, preaching and wow, there turned out to be massive amounts of talk. This is back in the heyday of huge radio preachers. I also studied like a fiend the countless different sects of Christianity right down to the bone. The good, bad and ugly. I dabbled in the study of other world religions, but only an overview. Two thousand years of east and west Christianity filled enough of my synapsis to keep my mind in constant movement. I only tapped a small well of and endless supply of an extremely fascinating history built from the son of an obscure carpenter in a fledgling community, people asked, "Could anything good come out of there?"

Billions of "FOLLOWERS," over centuries, with countless splits, horrifying wars, corruption, slavery, with some much powerful, undeniable great lifesaving, eternal good.

Mind boggling incongruency.

All this study, investigation, input, information, history, fascinating wild doctrines, helped for a season to stay off the affliction and depression, but over time and now with time for reflection, I know I polluted myself in an almost irreconcilable way.

A very potent drug. Maybe as bad as all the illegal drugs I smoked, snorted and ingested.

No going back to have a redo. No way I can wash my mind clean. A new and significant battle, is threatening to undo my path to stability and normality.

Hearing sect driven interpretation of biblical principles, philosophies, creeds and doctrines causes difficulty in me.

This mainly comes from homilies and sermons. At this point, I have chosen to apply a prohibition against, hearing any religious opinions or interpretation. When I hear an incredibly deep, or ignorantly shallow interpretation or insight, coming from truly sincere and honorable servants, my mind fills with half a dozen of other doctrinal positions on the subject.

Until I can come to a place where I can hear, without having the, *sounds good, maybe, could be, what about* and three other interpretations, all in a matter of seconds, I am under prohibition.

The night of transition, on my way to the hospital, TO GET CHECKED OUT, before I checked in, I pulled out a sheet paper I tapped out on a keyboard a few weeks before my crack up. With a bit of anxiety, I printed it out, stuffed in my pocket more than excited to share the over load of religious information I polluted myself under. Looking back, I have no idea, why I needed to share this with two of the seven so badly, before I went into the hospital, and I have deep regrets.

With shaky hands and clipped, racing speech, I stuttering out the typed words. All of it came in incomplete sentences and difficult translated words. If a random stranger found the paper and read the chicken scratches, they would have seen and heard a tiny wooden bird springing from a clock on the wall, declaring, Cuckoo. Cuckoo. Cuckoo.

Since that time, I have spent time to bring it to a place of continuity, but much remains clipped and it would take too long to explain all the meanings of the phrases, but I will try to illustrate the second area I polluted myself with.

Religious Doctrines.

Here is the updated version, from a less volatile and more reflective place.

I have listened to at least 6370 sermons and teachings since 1983 if not more. Plus, all the ones I listened to on the radio each day for years. Walter Martin, called the Bible Answer Man. Dr. James Dobson, from Focus on the Family. Chuck Swindoll, Charles Stanley, John Macarthur, Harold Camping, J. Vernon McGee, plus many, many others for years.

In 1964 I found myself born into a super-duper Catholic family. From my earliest memory, I recall kneeling every night in front of a huge painting of Jesus, saying the "Hail Mary" and the "OUR FATHER." We went to MASS more than weekly, then, at six years of age, we moved from an extended family with fame and honor in the land of ten thousand lakes to the land of fruits and nuts, literally that was the name for Sunnyvale California.

I went as they led me through the Stations of the Cross under Catholic teaching. So much so I felt sadness because a girl I liked early on happened to be a Protestant, I did not know which sect, I only knew I could not marry her. This became an ancient place of grief under religious indoctrination. Memory tells me this is back in the third grade.

I received my first holy communion, went through the catechism and confirmation, neither of which I understood in the slightest. I continued to go off and on to Mass, but never listened. Then we mostly stopped. Mom being in and out of the mental hospitals.

At the age of nineteen I went through the one step program and I believed in Jesus for my salvation. I attended an Assemblies of God church with roots in Pentecost. They taught we owe God ten percent of our income, coming down to the alter to GET SAVED, speaking in tongues, the Baptism of the Holy Spirit and other miracle working gifts are alive and well today.

I will give parts of the clipped list of the numerous movements and philosophies, with slight explanation. I am the one who agreed to get into, study, listen and debate. My mind feels like a server bay connected to every single one of these wide reaching and, at times contradictory positions. In an instance with no need for a search bar, several divergent teachings with immediate recall blink with sharp clarity.

I allowed myself to interact in a significant way with each of these.

A long, wide and diverse list.

Christ life: Freedom, Christ in you the hope of glory. Grace not works.

Anti-Baptist teachings: Mennonites and Amish. Choose to follow God.

Calvinism: Reformed theology, doctrine is big, Sola Scriptura, Synods. God chooses only some and hates the rest. No spiritual gifts today.

Inner healing teaching: Issue driven, internal wounds, boundaries, don't live in denial. Go back and see in your mind Jesus there and let him heal the wound.

Daily Life: The corporate church is corrupt, (Leavened). Encourage each other daily, not once a week.

Renewal: Toronto blessing. The Father's blessing. Fire tunnels, drunk in the spirit, slain in the spirit. The supernatural gifts of God are practiced, seen and expected.

Charismatic: Raise your hands, sing chorus, believe it the gifts of the Spirit, but not always.

Evangelical: You're a sinner, repent, accept Jesus as your personal savior.

Eastern Orthodoxy: Liturgy, dessert father's, ecumenical counsels, icons. An unbroken tradition with mysticism as a core.

Seventh day Christians: Sabbath on Saturday, do not eat animal flesh.

Farther Heart Teaching: FATHER is the reason the Son came and died, to bring us to FATHER.

Restoring the foundations: Go back and address all the places and say some magic words.

YWAM: Thousands of young people being discipled for three months and then go on a three-month mission's trip to another country.

Seeker Sensitive: Make people feel comfortable so they can hear the message.

Those are some "Movements," I spent many hours in, and with. Here is a list of numerous philosophies I also marinated under.

I am well-seasoned.

Raising the dead, praying for the sick, God's voice, the presence of the LORD, fellowship, the purpose driven church, healing crusades, evangelical crusades, God is not willing any should parish, God only chooses the elect, End Time prophecy, rapture, Prophets and Apostles for today, Revival, Reformation, Transformation, grafted in Christians, head coverings, prophetic words, demons living in believers, yes, no, maybe so, home church vs corporate, governing board, elders, deacons, women teaching in church, church board of directors, heavy metal Christian music, contemporary Christian music, HYMNS only, Gospel music, WORSHIP, hands raised, drums in church, spiritual songs, liberal churches, conservative churches, new churches, church splits, home schooling, anti-vaccine, growing kids God's way, train up a child, king James is the only bible, eating meat, drinking wine, the church is a family, join the church, become a member of the church, pay your tithe so you don't steal from God, give as you prosper not from compulsion or a grudge, the framework, biblical counseling, Christian counseling, inner healing counseling.

God HELP ME!

Is there still a pure baby in all this contradictory polluted bath water? I hear many alternating opinions on this sad question.

Jesus is not selfish. If the church wanted HIM to watch teachings on biblical principles nonstop, which would He choose? All, everyone? How could a consensus materialize? A simple majority of all the different sects or two thirds?

This pollution came at my own hand with big open ears and willing participation. I dealt with the conflict in several different ways. Provocative statements, tuning people out, putting people in a box. These are wrong, deadly wrong, and I regret my words, actions and attitudes.

The next area where I polluted myself over lapped with Doctrinal Pollution in many ways and in the same rough timeframe.

Manic Life Pollution.

Acting on ideas I thought up, starting business, saying yes, all the time, listening to the problems of others, buying properties, overload of giving, taking massive financial risk, self-sacrifice and self-denial, all became a powerful drug to keep my mind oiled against the dark threat waged at war with my life in the crosshairs.

Sure, on several, well more the several occasions, I fell into a dark funk with real, tricky, persuasive power falling over me at certain times and I fell as a silent, distant, deaf mute, but BING, BANG, BOOM, I snapped out of it, ZING, right back to crazy manic living. Usually a day or two, the longest turned out to be the worst week of my life and I fully detached from reality, but I broke out as if nothing happened. A prequel to more serious coming events.

I will go over some highlights of my mid-range life experience. I will work to chronologically add many of the whiplash actions without going down too many rambling tangents or dead ends. I will leave out names and dates. You know, TO PROTECT THE INNOCENT. I hope to lay out the interconnected parts. I will mention, with a degree of anticipation, I hope this will turn out to be beneficial written, form of talk therapy instead of a trap.

Twenty-five to fifty-five years.

The city I have lived in for the last three decades, should have only been a stomping ground for a year. After a biblical training program, then it was off overseas to work under a missionary for two years, back to the States for ORDINATION and assignment to THE FIELD forever. Plentiful harvest field, not enough laborers.

A sad reality.

I came to a clear and undeniable truth. I would be a crappy, pastor, missionary, servant. I might have done well with vision casting, but I do not have the gift to Shepard those in need. I have met a few who have the gift. Very few. Most church leaders are administrators and brilliant motivational speakers. Actual Pastors, true Shepard's over the souls of many, are nearly an extinct rare breed.

Instead of the ministry I went to work for an old line mutually held insurance company, selling life insurance. I stood ignorant to a fact it seemed everyone knew; selling life insurance is one step above pond scum. I took it well and did my best and found I held a gift. I held so few abilities, with less than zero education, and no money, so this became a solid value.

Selling an intangible product is not an easy task. Plus, they are one offs, and you had to meet people at night as they worked in the day. So, I reached out to employers who already paid for group health insurance, dental, vision and group term life. The employers benefit package, BENEFITS. If I could sell the benefit package, then I would have one employer client and all the employees as well, then I could pitch life insurance to all of them.

Worked like a charm. Better in fact.

Like a rocket ship, my income went from just above the gutter to the satisfier, plus I became massively busy. I loved it. Up, up, and away. I bought a nicer car, five acres of land to build a house on, oops banks don't lend to commission only sales folks until you have two years of proof. Crap. Oh well, I found an investor to go in on a duplex with me. I lived in one side and managed the rental on the other. A great deal and wouldn't you know the value went up quick as Lickety Split. Plus, the great blessing. The first of the Perfect Seven came into existence there.

New tract homes were going up all around, why not get a brand spanking new sweet place? The second of the seven came smiling to life in the new house. I continued marketing, selling and enrolling group benefit packages all around. During this time, I filled my free mind time in doctrinal pollution.

Then from nowhere, an enormous door opened. Two Health Maintenance Organizations, HMOs, came to town. HMO's did not have an excellent reputation to say the least. An enormous benefit in my direction. Most of the Group Health Brokers held an unfavorable and ignorant view of the HMO's fresh arrival on our door step.

These two HMO's, were not run in some dark room, by un-ethical, unfeeling, cigar smoking, fat cats. Turns out these were run and owned by the local doctors, who created groups and confirmed best treatment, best practice. Local doctors made the decisions.

Lower cost and higher benefits.

I went to all the largest employers and stayed constantly busy.

Incredible.

Why not build a big house on some acreage? Why not in-deed?

The third, fourth, fifth, sixth and seventh came as unde-served miracles in the big blue house out in the country. Best years of my life. The Beautiful Perfect Seven all under one roof.

Nothing is better.

I dedicated my whole heart to their care, safety, and protec-tion. Bless them. The greatest of all. At that point I should have been content, but my mind would not settle.

I added a few side hobbies while I raised the seven and ran the brokerage business. I could not stop. For three decades al-most every idea, vision, popping in my mind, needed action. It did not matter if success seemed tangible or not, I acted with enthusiasm as a defense or maybe an offensive mechanism to keep at bay the enemy of my soul.

Here are a few. They all were side business or hobbies and a few long-term revenue producers.

I wrote a book late at night, and into the wee hours of the morning, then I found a company to print it with PERFECT BINDING. From the beginning to the end the process was very gratifying. This is before self-publishing and I held no interest in getting published, I only wanted to hold the thing in my hand. The joy I found in writing filled me to overflowing. I paid to have two hundred and fifty printed and when I went to get the box, fluttering butterflies of excitement flapped through my heart. I gave them all away. A great experience, then it ended.

I created a small prescription drug discount program and started to sell it across the country then I felt convicted as most of those buying the card were widows, or older women, so I gave the card away for free. Weird how people will pay money, but FREE does not go over well.

The HMO's left my area and left me with thousands of employees to move to tradition health insurance plans which cost more with fewer benefits, so I started a company to administer Health Reimbursement Arrangements, HRA, and Health Savings Accounts, HSA. They set these up alongside a high deductible health plan. This is back in the very early days when they called them Consumer Directed Health Plans, CDH. I lost money on this endeavor for five years. Roll the dice. So, I purchased a commercial building large enough to house the few employees who worked for me at the time plus the multitudes to come, as the company exploded in the growth my mind anticipated, envisioned and dreamed. By the skin of my teeth, I made it to profitability, then I lost interest, so I stated a small Software as a Service company, SAS, and dumped more money than I had to get it from an embryotic thought to actual products in this material world. Then the writing on the wall made me shut it down in shame and sadness. A year later it resurrected and became a profit center, than I lost interest.

Not to worry, I had a new idea.

DING, DING!

I started three online stores and had them loaded with over one hundred thousand products. This is the early days of drop shipping. My thought bend to not having to touch or hold inventory, have great products and generate revenue from volumes of sales, so I made my mark up very low. Sales came flooding in, the only problem I lived naïve. I did not for the life of me, think there were so many thieves out there who had other people's credit cards. A very unsettling reality. I am no zealot so I returned any funds I even considered suspect. Too many to count. No problem, then I got creamed. I pushed all three stores onto Amazon and could not believe all the products showed up and offered so far and wide so easily. Off to the races. WHAM, I sold eighty-five Xbox consoles in a matter of hours. I set a five percent markup over the wholesale price I needed to pay, so I knew I would be competitive, but the feed sent to Amazon contained the wrong info. The prices did not match the product. Mine showed a Xbox for Twenty-eight dollars. Crap. I turned the site off and refunded nearly a hundred people. A day later my name became worse than mud. If you see a seller with a ninety-two score and another with a ninety-eight, you tend to go with the higher one. My score became ZERO and fast. No coming back from there.

FORGET-ABOUT-IT.

Worse than mud.

Oh well, I had other ideas. The declaration of my life.

While the administration firm and SAS company needed oversight with massive expense and almost enough revenue, I went into television. I created twelve thirty minutes television programs because I had the idea. Then I bought into a local low power antilog station and took it from one analog station to four digital channels. One of the greatest times of business vision and down in the dirt nuts and bolts, then I lost interest, and the world shook with significate quacking and a global downturn.

They called it the GREAT RECESSION.

An understatement.

In reality, an undeniable issue shined with simplicity.

The government wanted home ownership, so they set up a deal to sell very expense insurance to cover the down payment most people cannot come up with, so the mortgage brokers, could do desk top underwriting for people to get their first home or refinanced their current mortgages with a negative amortized thirty-year mortgage, and then they sold those crappy mortgages and bundled them together with back up insurance, and the piper came calling, the chickens came home to roost, and millions suffered, but the government bailed the whole thing out by buying its own paper, and other debt, gave the insurance company billions to cover the unconscionable loses and made all the scoundrels whole, for their despicable, criminal and abhorrent business practices, too big to fail, don't ya know, and the whole world suffered.

But interest rates were low and banks needed to unload the inventory of crappy loans and were more than happy to make deals. This fact opened a door to my ridiculous mind.

All the while I juggled all the other parts of the businesses, the seven and life itself, I thought each of the seven could own a house of their own. If I cosigned, they only needed a paycheck. The first worked at Dairy Queen, the second as a janitor, the third at a café. Off to the races, and a trifecta existed. Nineteen fifties interest rates, nineteen nineties home prices, and the bank would bend over backward to make it happen. Because these loans were FHA, the government made requirements, and the banks paid. New roof, dishwasher, flooring, all the terminate work, they even paid to have one of the houses repainted and agreed to pay closing costs. More than a trifecta. The government allowed all this ciaos to transpire as they bailed out the too big to fails, so I felt more than happy, to see the first three of the beautiful seven as home owners, plus it kept me busy.

Busy, busy, busy.

A perfect way to keep me from falling off the mental cliff.

Then I started an ultra-low-end film production company, and movie distribution entity while I wrote eight screen plays. This may have been the one authentic place for my mind to rise above the clouds with more than enough input than I needed. Only problem, I had other issues to engage in. The Seven needed oversight and help, the commercial building came due for refinance, I made a deal for a large portion of my adminis-tration firm with a bigger entity, and the employees I cared so much for, went on to new horizons.

I found myself all alone.

Not a good place.

As I made a deal to unload a large portion of the admin-istration firm, shut down the film production, give back the television station, sold the office building, stopped writing and came home, with two small internet-based companies I could run all alone, I needed to come to grips with my wheely ways.

A million miles an hour to an all stop.

Not good. Not at all.

Without preparation or guidance, I found myself untethered, flapping in the wind, away from my go to mechanisms and fallback positions, all alone and unequipped.

A stranger in an unknown land.

The beginnings of an emotional breakdown, coming unglued, started with a surreal power and tricky temptation. It started slow at first then picked up speed until I found myself bulldozed under the onslaught.

When you dream up, and act out on, the most wild and crazy ideas, roll the dice and place a bet with all your resources for three decades and then come to a screeching halt, it seems fair to conclude difficulty may ensue.

An understatement.

Darkness, accusation, lies and deception came in with one goal to overtake my sanity, turn me to mush and detach me from reality. For a slight season it worked out well for the accuser, but those days are over, in the rearview, a blip on the radar of life, a painful struggle, with potent recognition, but by no means a fateful defeat. Anything but.

Good ridden.

I have come out on the other side with a fair bit of understanding and recognition of the enemy attacking me and a balanced plan to walk in stability, day by day.

Internal voices are only the playground, an embryonic sandbox without real weapons or power. Like a breeze flowing through a screen door, unless you give notice, ask questions and debate. Let the wispy powerless words pass by and fall on deaf ears. Easier said than done, but worth the effort and an important counter measure I am still working to refine.

GOD of Heaven?

The maker understands the battle and has given defensive weapons and a few offensive ones to stand firm and combat the deceptive arrows flung haphazardly against my very existence. One tool in the quiver is to look beyond and not engage in the multitude of rambling thoughts bombarding me and look the other way. I can let loose and pour out, as an illustration of how my mind rolls, and I could have gone on for pages and then some. Part of my healing. My move toward stability and balance is to NOT let these thought patterns take root and produce an unhealthy harvest. It is not a simple task as I have dabbled, wrestled and fought these argumentative, worthless diatribes for years. I am not in control of and have very little authority over, the onslaught of thoughts, so I work with a new found conviction to put off, look over, and not engage in the mind war.

I can do nothing about random off the wall, fly-by-night thoughts. They come without notice, and many are valueless, so there is no actual need to engage, defend, combat or even acknowledge their existence. The big ones, like the LIE intermixed with the STRUGGLE to comprehend all the incomprehensible parts of life, nature, existence, have so many twisted branches and interconnected webs, I need to be on guard and aware at any moment's notice. If it goes too far, I have three who I am accountable to and they are available so I can share without concern and get the muck out before it digs in and goes too far. This simple option eluded me for most of my life, but now and going forward I will not hold hidden deceptions and downright nutty thoughts to myself. The light of confession has proven to be a valuable tool to extinguish the darkness and keep it from digging in and finding a place to hide away for future assault.

If I didn't stay busy for so long, I could have possibly seen the value of safe ears to open up to and verbally confess some crazy goings on in me. Looking back always brings about a clear focus and can contain actual future value.

Learn from back then to the benefit of the yet to come.

That being said, I am going to go all the way back, to the beginning. I am not sure how this will go.

Born on a Pogo Stick.

I do not remember being born and taking my first breath. Most memories start at about four years or so and others were stories told to me I resonate with. One underlining theme in memory and the tales told, rings true.

I was a super bouncy kid.

I felt like I lived on the tips of my toes with a constant up and down bounce and an overwhelming need to talk and talk and talk. A Yippy Yapper bouncing on a pogo stick. Latent memories and detailed verbal accounts with the need for a bit of introspective interpretation inter-layered for a well-rounded explanation of my upbringing are as much of a sound truth as can be expected. Most of those who were there back then, are dead or lived looking thorough their own young eyes at the big bad world out there so all I can do is connect my own memories to the stories told. I will do my best. Our memories are our own, no other entity holds claim, nor can they make a quantified accusation or defense.

Memories belong to us.

Verbal Accounts.

My earliest remembrance starts after the first four stories told with humor about my young days. The first is a time I have no recollection of, it starts with, "I could not figure out how, at three years old, he got out, every day when I put him down for a nap so I waited and watched. The little scamp closed his eyes like a sleeping bug for several minutes then he hopped out of bed and pulled the curtain rod off, went to the door and used the rod to unclip the snap hook from the door. He put the rod back in place and sneaked out." The laughter over the story never brought about the slightest recognition of the event but told a tale. I did not like to sleep in the day.

The next story went like this. "He does not like going to church. He got stitches in his noggin two Saturdays in a row. Slammed his head against the radiator in the hallway one week and bashed his head against the kitchen table the next. The boy can't sit still and does not understand what is around him." Twenty stitches in total on my three-year-old coconut head.

The next two stories were told with the loudest laughter and good nature from my father who is far and away one of the greatest men ever to live, bar none. I can still see in my mind's eye his face and wonderful enthusiasm as he shared his recollection of the events. He took a Sunday afternoon nap on the couch putting his glasses, wallet, keys and watch on the coffee table. When he woke up, he called out, "J. Clement, if you were a pair of glasses, keys, and wallet where would you go." The story goes, I placed my three-year-old hand in his and took him out the back door, down the alley, across the street up the next alley to a stranger's garage. There on a shelve behind some boxes, were the items. I have no recollection, but I still hear his contagious laugh.

An OUTSTANDING melodic song of pure joy.

The next tale I have some slivers of memory of.

Orange Paint, Turpentine and Laughter.

For some unexplained reason I got into my tiny four-year-old mind, the need for my father's dark green car to go through a makeover with a brighter color. I somehow found a gallon of paint, carried it to the street with a large brush, got on my bare knees and slather bright orange paint across the driver's side door. I got busted. A neighbor called out for my father and before I made it too far, I found myself in the cement wash tub in the basement and the smell of Turpentine as my father scrubbed the orange from my fingers, face and arms. To this day the smell of the toxic fluid fills me with a fondness.

Odd but true.

Not an inch of anger from my father. I think he must have been able to get the wet paint off without much difficulty or permanent damage to his car, but I never found out those details. Love, acceptance, far reaching encouragement are my only remembrance of my father for my whole life with him. Not to worry, there turned out to be a great deal of discipline from my mother. Discipline may be the wrong definition. From an obscure place, out of nowhere, at a moment's notice, the environment would shift in a big way. BING, my ear would receive a pinch, twist and pull, or a she scrubbed a bar of soap over my tongue with vigor and fury, back and forth until I gagged. This was the discipline for saying, stupid or shut up. Taking the Lord's name in vain brought the tabasco sauce out and not for just one, two or three drips on the tongue, more like half the bottle, and let me be clear, it burned right down to the bone. My head feels a tingling just thinking about it to this day. I still do not add much spice to my meal. Besides soap and hot sauce on the tongue, a hair brush, yard stick, ruler or wooden spoon became the go to as the instrument to inflict pain against the back side. I can see now, in my mind's eye back then, I lingered internally with very little peripheral insight to the goings on outside and around me. So, most of the infliction held very little value in behavioral change. A sad truth. I did not understand the reason, the anger, bulging veins in the neck, red face, the suffering and the words such as, "what is wrong with you? How come you can't be like everyone else? Don't you see how hard you are? Just listen and do what you are told."

More like declarations than actual questions. I get it, frustration should be a key emotional component when you are unable to control another human being especially a small, kind of odd one. I hold no blame in my heart, or desire to explain away my nature. At the same time, I will not go to the commonly fallback position, MY MOTHER had a HARD CHILDHOOD, or the big one, this is the cause of my current struggles what I went through as a child? My mother never punched me in the face, kicked me or threw me down the stairs, put a hot iron against my face or put my head in a vice grip. She did slap me with an open hand and it left a welt, but the quintessential definition of abuse does not resonate in my faded memories. It could be denial, a protection mechanism, a self-guided side track and all the other shit people with degrees puke out because they are in the same boat as everyone else, maybe WORSE. My issues today, were the same ones back then, and it did not change from getting my butt spanked. My mind has been this way since it formed. Environment did not create it, maybe hereditary infused DNA, but who cares, no one can change the womb they grew in, nor the color of the eyes you get or the size, shape, and hue of your body. Get a glue, no one can go back into the womb, flip a coin and come out different.

Just the facts.

I love my mother, long since dead now, but in the same breath I pity her and feel a great deal of sadness for her short, seventy years of existence on this unbelievable spinning tiny, but massive sphere, floating and turning, twisting with some gravitational pull which by some mystical unintelligent, natural, survival of the fittest force, keeps the seasons coming in about the same date for centuries, flowing in perfect line, mathematically calculable. An awesome truth, but hey, we, as less they a tiny species, evolved and created technology powerful enough, through our greed, hubris and, well pick your definition, unsocial justice, inequity, are the changers of climate, let's say hairspray, Freon, diesel and unleaded exhaust. The climate changing species. The creators of bigger hurricanes and tornadoes, forest fires and earthquakes. Some say yes, others say no.

Does it make a difference?

Have we as a tiny, greedy, grubbing species caused it? Can We Fix It? Who knows? It appears there is a battle brewing with an unforeseen result. Survival of the fittest, or the climate may turn on a dime and ice age may head our way, like I had been told over and over throughout my young life. Maybe we will need to pollute more to keep the freezing cold from coming.

What does this have to do with soap on my tongue or wood across my butt? Only an illustration just how small we all are even though so many think they are big. My environment shaped me, but it did not create me. I came as I am, to a place I held no control over, at a time not from my choosing, intact as I am.

Glad to meet you.

With my father tilting the balancing scale all the way, and then some, toward the positive, the possible, the fantastic, certainly held a value for development, but not alteration of the core make up I came with. Sure, the drastic difference, of powerful hope and overflowing joy from my father to uncontrolled anger, bitterness and negativity on my mother's side, did have some impact.

No one could deny.

I have a tendency to small slivers of brilliance along with off the rocker swings of mental instability. A real issue, but most is biological, some environmental and a crap load is from the spiritual realm, so here I am. An individual, unique human being amongst billions of others without a desire to blame another. I am seeking help from others, but with a bit of skepticism, unless the anxiety moves to overdrive, then FORGET-ABOUT-IT. Knock me out and fill me to overflowing with a concoction of chemicals the government has deemed to be legal and a few others on the side. Until then I will keep moving forward to a place of balance, stability and longevity.

Until the age of six I lived in the house my grandfather, on my mother's side, build in south Minneapolis. My mother being the youngest of seven, married my father, who bought her childhood home, and I turned out to be the fifth child out of six, and the bouncy one.

With a big promotion, and a huge opportunity, we moved from the safety, familiarity of a huge community in mid-west safety, security and normality, to Palo Alto near Stanford University. California is the place you need to be, so they loaded up the station wagon and moved to the soon to be named, Silicon Valley. My father drove to the big city of San Francisco every day, but I did not have a clue. We only lived there for a year and I went to kindergarten. This is nineteen sixty-nine, Vietnam, and hippies filled the newscasts, I did not watch or know about. There are four things I remember, which still affect me today from that transitional year.

A best Friend, Fun with God, Stories and Serial killers.

Two doors down lived a boy my same age, and we hit it off. His mother did arts and crafts and we went to kindergarten together. Same age, same name. My first best friend. We played, ate peanut butter and jelly sandwiches, drank soda, colored in coloring books and never fought. A great first friend and wonderful memory.

Two doors the other way lived an older couple who took our family under their wings. A sweet couple, but not Catholic. In fact, they were protestants who had a church for kids. I went several times, and it holds a memory of fun. Puppets, candy, songs and crafts. Fun, fun, fun, till your mama takes the church away.

"They are not Catholic, so you can't go."

It felt okay, because I went to a half day of school where we brought a blanket for nap time, ate fruit and nuts, drank apple juice, did crafts and listened as the teacher read a story out-load. A sweet memory. Listening as someone reads is one of the great joys of my life, and now you can download the digital voice.

Who says technology is not good?

These wonderful experiences became quickly over shadowed by a significant fear. The Zodiac Killer. My young mind had no grid to recognize this Bay Area killer did his dastardly deeds at a significant distance away from where this six-year-old lived and children were not on his hit list, but I shook with terror anyhow, most days and plenty of nights. They never caught the killer, so I lived with an unsettling worry for several years. Not sure why I told no one, I should have. The fear left as I grew up and gained understanding about life. I see my inability or reluctance to open up and talk became an area I need to overcome. Trouble ensues when I keep my thoughts hidden. It is also not healthy to puke out the wild and cooky to everyone, so I have the three I trust, who are for me without apprehension, and complete sincerity to help disarm the minefield of thought patterns I can easy stumble into.

A new and rather uncomfortable practice I am learning to fully engage in.

Dunnock.

From Palo Alto we moved down the expressway to Sunnyvale onto the greatest streets to grow up on, DUNNOCK WAY. The day our truck unloaded our stuff ten kids from the street were on our door step. Several were the age of my siblings and one my age, he became my second-best friend in life. Besides the welcoming party on that day, it turned out there were kids everywhere, literally, and all of them interacted in a natural and freewheeling ease. More than beautiful. With a quick calculation, forty kids lived on Dunnock, and they all got along with no conflicts. We road bikes, roller-skated, played football, baseball in the street, basketball on the drive way and had massive games of ditch. We swam in several pools on the block, with more than twenty kids coming and going with no invitation. No one stood alone, left out, an amazing and unique blessing I have never experienced again. Could have been an anomaly or just part of the times.

The first grade became a transition year. I still lived at night with the terror a knife wielding killer would take me out, but good things happened.

Walking, Love, and Reading.

I walked to school with my new best friend. He held a colorful metal box with a thermos and food. I gripped a brown paper bag. Never knew what Items his contained, but mine always contained three items. Sandwich, fruit and candy. Peanut Butter and jelly, bologna and cheese, tuna fish, egg salad, liver worse, made on bright white WONDER BREAD became the staple. An apple, orange, pear, green grapes acted as the health side and then a small, Snickers, Mars or Musketeer candy bar rounded out the hand-held lunch.

As we walked together to school, all our siblings walked in groups as well, then other kids would come out of their homes on the same course and path to elementary school. These became other friends who lived on other streets around the school, but only some of us were lucky enough to live on the best street in the neighborhood.

DUNNOCK WAY.

I still look back with a majestic memory to the one and only grade of school I enjoyed and seemed to excel in. I learned to read in the first grade and I fell in love, for one of a few times in my life. I fell hard and fast, head over heels, all in. Her name is Mrs. Reddington. She would be in her late eighties now, but back then in her mid-thirties, she smelt so good, with a soft voice, caring spirit and her absolutely beauty captivated me all the way. I could not get my mind off her, day or night. I dressed in my best clothes, sat straight, listened, and thoroughly enjoyed every minute I found myself lucky enough to be around my teacher.

Plus, she read stories to us.

Heaven.

My best friend, lived next store, but went to another first-grade class. His entire class flunked, held back to repeat the first grade over. Although we spent gobs of fun times together on Dunnock, at school we barley talked or interacted. Weird. The grade you were in somehow became a discriminating factor for social interaction, at least it turned out to be back then and there. Looking back, repeating the first grade may have done me well, no way to tell, all I know is, first grade is the only grade I think I completed with actual success.

Second grade came with an angry croaking frumpy man who did not smell good at all. Mean and impatient who did not enjoy children. Wrong profession buddy. If you flipped a coin to the other side, or shifted a magnetic field from ultra-positive and refreshing, to dark, scary, with extreme negativity, you would have a perfect illustration of the difference from first grade to second.

A real bummer.

Every chance I could I went to Mrs. Reddington's class, just for a glimpse, a wave and that smile which still makes my heart pound.

My third-grade teacher felt like the reincarnation of the Wicked Witch of the West, with a constant frown on her face and quick disciplinary tendency as her favored go to. She contained a stern toughness people praised, so I heard how lucky I was to sit under her tutelage. I did not concur, but somehow the scary, tough, leader of a secret conjurer's coven, transformed into Miss Maryann from Romper Room when it became story time. She loved to read to her little test subjects, and she held a significant gift. Different voices, perfect pauses, volume change, and she turned the book to the class to show the scattered pictures in the book. She waited and shifted the book so every eye could gaze upon the black and white sketches. I can still feel the excitement getting to see the illustrations along with all my other class mates with elbows on our tiny desks to get a peek.

Two other redeeming values manifested during third grade. The most beautiful girl in the whole wide world sat two seats in front of me to the right. I fell in deep lasting love the moment I first laid eyes on her. We never kissed or even held hands, but we went steady, whatever that means, for two years, I got to walk her home from school even though it was the opposite direction of mine. I did not care. We played together, that is what we called back then, playing. I road my bike to her house, ate dinner or lunch on weekends with her family. The most beautiful girl I ever met, then her father bought another house, and she moved.

My heart still feels remnants of the cracks from the brokenness.

That year I also got hooked into playing for a freshly established traveling sport no one in our neck of the woods ever heard of. SOCCER. In the early seventies not many kids in the

U.S. knew of the game or played soccer. The father of a friend of mine immigrated from Germany and he liked FOO BALL, as he called it, so he recruited me and a group of others third graders and formed a team. I could not really understand his rough broken English, but he taught us all to dribble, pass, kick, shoot and score and we did all the way to the championship. Soccer is a great way to burn the bouncy, hyper tendencies out of any kid. We traveled all over the bay area to play on weekends, practiced twice a week which helped me burn energy, learn a new skill and became an outlet of stability. Then summer came, and I started in little league baseball. Soccer in the winter, baseball in the summer, football on the street, basketball on the drive way. Sports activity held a strong value in keeping my zipping mind off the abnormal, plus it is enjoyable, even when you lose.

Fourth grade became the beginning of another transition. They put me in the dummies class. They called it the "A+ Program," got to love the bureaucrats. All the kids in the school knew the truth. The stupid kids are in that class. They even bused others from districts away to participate in the screwed-up experiment.

I cannot blame my environment or the cards dealt to me, or for my lack of ability to achieve in the confines of academia. Something in my mind did not work right. For the life of me, I could not pass the tests. I tried, and tried with the same result, failure, so I gave up and faked, cheated, lied and they moved me to the next grade. I used my ability of manipulative speech and a general likeable spirit, to put at ease the unionized public servants who hold a high calling in the education of developing human beings.

With my inability to fit in the mold of structured instruction, they moved me around with more experiments. An odd conglomeration of switching teachers, classes and structure all in the hope I would connect into a disconnected puzzle.

Bless their bleeding hearts.

An obscure answer or experiment came from some place out of my hearing. "Give the kid a high dose of a very low-cost drug." CAFFEINE. I had to drink a large cup of coffee in the morning, before school and then go to the teachers' lounge, twice a day, and chug a fizzy drink called TAB. Not sure they have this soda anymore. I understand the carbonated drink contained an exorbitant amount of caffeine and no sugar. Pound the hyper kid with caffeine seems counterproductive, but who am I to argue. I obediently followed the odd instruction, plus I got to know all the teachers. Even though I bounced like a jitter bug on a pogo stick, I could talk, and verbally engage from a natural inquisitive interest, so the instructors let their hair down behind closed doors. I sipped my drink slow and learned some juicy gossip, which I kept to myself, in a secret place, to enjoy in my wide imagination. Two were having an affair and got married. Oh, the scandal.

I continued the daily ritual of caffeine infusion through the seventh grade. I guess they have more sophisticated drugs for hyper kids, ACHD is now the name used for the new generation. Not sure the benefits outweigh the effects. Doesn't matter, as long as bouncy kids sit still as calm robotic zombies.

Oh, the way of the world.

I could read, thanks to Mrs. Reddington in first grade, although I could not comprehend the meaning. If someone read to me, I contained a strong, clear comprehension and could retain the message with a profound ability to repeat it back almost verbatim. No way to go through life needing a personal reader attached to your hip, plus the cost is prohibitive. My mind zipped around in such a continual, spiraling disconnected, detached place, I could not comprehend the meaning of words I read. I would try to study, but in the end, the words I read as questions on the test and the four possible answers, twisted me in confusion without the slightest understanding. Sweat would rise and start pouring out above my eyebrows with anxiety and worry soaking my internal organs. Then an increased tension would ensue as I looked around the class watching as number two pencils filled in the little egg-shaped circles of A, B, C or D, so I applied my pencil lead and rapidly filled in the answer sheet in scattered patterns. A monkey can get twenty-five percent out of pure guessing. I did worse than your average monkey. I should have just answered "A," to every question and I may have hit a higher mark.

When someone told a story or read to me, then I focused in without effort. I can listen to an audible book, newscast, and a movie all at the same time with pretty good retention, but reading a test question, searching for the correct answer, still makes me sweat. Good thing real life, work, friendships, family, risk taking, do not come with the need to read questions and guess the answer. It is also good, nowhere in society, do you sit with thirty others of your own age, from different skill sets, back rounds, gifts, abilities, weaknesses, all learning the same exact thing with the sure cure way to quantify results. Checking marks on a paper. Oh wait, except in this brilliant experiment they call public school. A system which still lets the kids out for summer, so they can help with THE HARVEST. Just one shining light of the archaic system which needs billions more of funding.

I do not blame the administrators, teachers or system itself, for my inability to fit my twisty tourney brain into the square peg of academic achievement. It is not their fault. Many worked very diligently on my behalf and I am thankful for their kind service and sacrificial acts. My brain did not work the way they had constructed the system. Thank God I somehow learned to read, write and cypher, even though I cannot pass a test.

A good trade off.

As I struggled through the sixth grade, I still played sports year-round, interacted with many diverse people. Ages, ethnicities, religious upbringing, world views, the complete gambit. None of us cared. We did not hold to creeds, covenants, or small-minded philosophies. If you were Black or White, Asian, Hispanic, it did not matter in the slightest. All we cared about went to the core. Are you trustworthy? Will you narc, spill your guts and give the enforcement agents enough to take down others who did what we all did.

Plain and simple. Everyone knew the deal and looked beyond any outward differences. We actually joked about the differences. Now a days this is considered taboo, not back than. It brought laughter and good-natured fun.

Times have changed.

This is when I found myself introduced to illegal substances. Although a bit younger than most, easily two thirds of those a few years older all smoked pot, snorted crank and cocaine, took acid and ate mushrooms, just to name the top five. Far and away the vast majority partook. Those who abstained became the outsiders. The Goody-Two-Shoes. The rest of us were not dabblers. NO, we were morning, noon and night active participants. Interesting enough very few of the pot smoking, druggies did not do well in school. Many graduated early and succeeded in some large tech companies in the Silicon Valley. I can still hear conversations of how friends would say, "I was so wasted on the day of the big test and I aced it." The pointy headed sociologists, may want to study this incongruent issue to find how in the world this could be true. If we all failed in school and turned out to be complete losers, no surprise, but just the opposite happened. There are some of us burn-outs who dropped out, and drug use certainly could be a contributing factor, but not in my case. I dropped out from sure boredom and my absolute inability to succeed in the square box system.

Junior high came with an eye-opening experience, actually three.

SEX, DRUGS and ROCK & ROLL.

Drugs were everywhere and massive parties happened nearly every weekend. Someone's parents went out of town and dozens and dozens of teenage kids showed up and it became an off the charts wild party. Blaring fantastic music, enough alcohol to kill fifty elephants with experimental sex all around. Unbelievable. Next week another house where the parents left for a respite and bingo, SEX, DRUGS and ROCK & ROLL. I do not remember very many weekends where, within a ten-mile radius, one of these bashes did not take place. Being too young to drive did not matter, everyone became welcome to squeeze in.

No seat belt laws back then, so pack in.

I still struggle in recollection to come into a balanced agreement with the fact all of us back then, got shit faced all the time, week by week and still achieved success. Blows my mind. Most days the majority of us existed in a tweaked intoxicated state and still came out the other side with an ability to go on to succeed in big ways. Very big ways. I could never explain this weird anomaly. It is an unspoken secret. I choose to open it up with a hope to find a place of stability, balance, longevity in these written words. I will not speak for those back then, but the ones who still love me will understand, the others have their own journey to travail. May God help them. I am only one of many. So many little kids in a strange shifting world. We can all say the same phrase. SEX, DRUGS, and ROCK & Roll.

A pitiful, but strong statement. One with power and utter sadness.

I am very thankful for all those who experienced this up-bringing, quasi debauchery and difficult unexplainable transition as we share a common memory. We hold an unholy alliance, but a true-blue connection which shifted decades later with, the unanswered question, WHAT in the WORLD?

I could have used vulgarity there, but I held back.

Words are powerful, but emotions hold a greater power. A deep unexplainable power. The old farts now, but kids back then, around me, understand. A quandary which lacks explanation with an odd understanding.

A Painful truth.

I believe in God and more than a majority do not. It makes sense to me and I honor, most, but let me say with a twinkle in my eye, NOT ALL.

Around this point in my life, the phrase "MOM is SICK" became a common well used statement. Looking back, I understand this issue had been around for some time, years in fact.

The first time Mom went into the hospital my small mind only thought about death not mental illness. My only experience with hospitals had been when we went back to the "TWIN CITIES" and stayed at our cousin's house. My mother's sister, my aunt, lived in a hospital bed for a few months while several sets of cousins all played together. Breast cancer is the diagnosis, which for some odd reason, I had no clue. Cancer? No one told me. I woke up one morning to the sound of the whole house wailing with tears of unbelievable grief. I cringe at the memory of the most horrible sound I ever heard in all my life. A few months later my mom laid in a hospital bed and my tiny mind could not deal with the horror. I kept the tormenting thoughts to myself until I burst.

"I don't want my mom to die."

Mental illness does not kill, but the hospital looks just like the place those with cancer stay.

"Mom needs to rest. She will be home soon. Don't worry."

I did anyway.

That first lockdown happened years before the neighborhood went from adolescent to well-practiced, experimentalists in a broad spectrum of illegal substances and remained off the radar of my thoughts. I can never forget the second mental hospital stay as it has become a large dividing line in my existence. Not only the length of time she needed hospitalization, but the months and month of recovery at home, which would be worth the struggle if in the end no more need for inpatient stays or a stable dose of factory manufactured mind altering medication.

No. Many more stays and truck loads of potent prescriptions were on the horizon of treatment.

A bony sunken eyed tormented zombie swallowing gobs of chemical as a helping hand.

My heart breaks for my mother, and I would have done more, so much more, knowing what I know now. She suffered alone in a huge changing world without the life skills and assistance she deserved. Chemical intervention became the treatment, and it did not prove effective. For the next thirty years she lived under an evil tormenting shadow, waging war with frail weapons and she lost, big time. I could have, should have, done more, or at least sat down and listened. There is no excuse I can muster for not being there for her in her time of need and struggle. Of course, I was only a young self-focused boy when it started so I do not live with condemnation, for my time back then, but I do hold a profound painful regret in all the times I did nothing and the judgement I held tight in my heart towards her for so many years after.

Shame on me.

God bless my mother. Bless her soul.

Now a decade down the river of life from when she went to meet her maker, I find myself twisting in the wind with some similar and other abnormal mental issues, psychological diffi-culties, and strange foreign torments.

Oh, the irony. The cosmic joke lacking any comedic under-tones. I do not find even a miniscule of laughter in the revela-tion of shared torment. There is not any comfort in the knowl-edge of a hidden connection of a screwed-up mind although in this bright and shiny technological age, there is a provision of an endless supply of options.

I am using one, which is proving to bring some rewards, talk therapy in written form.

Hunting and pecking, here.

Seventh grade uprooted me from a single classroom where I could sit and do nothing all day but follow the paths of my broad imagination while, THE TEACHER, drowned on. Same desk, same room, same instructor all day then, WOWEE, four elementary schools got crammed into a single grade where we switched desks, class rooms systematically based on the clock. A time piece, ringing a bell as a loud declaration screeching to all the little minds full of mush to stand, walk, go to a locker and make your way to the next under sized desk, sit and listen until the next bell went off. I realize I said I never passed a class or test since way back in early elementary school, which is true, except the brilliant concept of ELECTIVES.

I succeeded in the fun classes.

I choose two elective classes and they were fabulous. English, grammar, science, math, became a familiar place of utter failure, but I succeeded in the personal choice programs. Home Economics and Stickery, plus Physical Education, PE.

Most of the guys I knew mocked me for picking feminine electives.

"Who is in auto mechanics and lapidary with you?" I asked with a sinister mock in my voice.

They named all the stinky, sweaty, arrogant boys in their elective choices.

"Who is Home EC and Stickery?" I asked.

Bingo.

The look on those, testosterone infused, tough guys pimpled faces, still shines brightly in my memory.

Brilliant.

I liked girls, all of them. They looked great, smelled wonderful, were soft and nice, plus they were more than enthusiastic to help a poor boy out. I became the class pet, and I milked my ignorance in both cooking and needlepoint to the max and it paid off in spades at least from my side. I failed all my other classes, except PE. I am still flabbergasted with a cynical amazement the keepers of keys of education moved me forward to the next grade.

"Let the others deal with the kid, we have too many other issues to take time to get to the bottom of failure. The union might ask us to strike and walk the picket lines until the STATE ponies up a few more breadcrumbs."

The way of public education.

It did not matter. Time to pack up and go somewhere else lifted its continual head over the horizon of life and lingered for years as a clanging sad continual cymbal. "Mom is sick, we are moving. Pack up," became as common as the changes in season. Almost on the dot. Every six months. Public schools have no choice, they have to take in any stray cat left on their doorstep, but I gave up long before, so I cut. A better word may be prohibition against classroom sitting, but cut is what we called it back in the day. I cut every class after only a few days. I knew if I did not show up on the first day, issues and questions would arise. After a couple days of sitting through each period, no one raised an eyebrow.

I never went back.

Got to love overloaded bureaucrats who used paper enrollment without an ability to hone down. Truancy could be an issue, KIDS HAVE to be in SCHOOL, so I became an expert in remaining invisible on the streets on school days. "My mom is sick" became my first go to if asked. Interesting enough many concerned citizens asked.

Bless their hearts.

Zing, Zap, Bing, POW, we moved to the ocean, ninth grade. Second half back to Sunnyvale. First half of tenth in MINNESOTA, then second back to the bay area in bright shining crystal California where we moved a couple of times and I stopped school altogether. A drop out. All in all, I sat in a high school classroom no more than a few dozen times.

This period of life became an unhealthy, and down right, destructive season with sharp dangerous arrows piercing my very life over and over. It is my fault, no one else's. From sixteen to eighteen could easily, hands down, be the worst time of my life. I crashed two cars and went to jail twice. One for drunk driving, the other for public belligerence and drugs plus many others debaucheries I will not go into at this time. The list could go on and on without end. I have a concern for the value in open sharing, specifics and details, may cause more harm than health, so I will stick to the crashes, jail and DUI.

From the ocean at Santa Cruz to the Silicon Valley is about thirty-five miles over an extremely tight, twisty mountain road they called a highway. More like a death trap, especially when you're wasted. Many weekdays and some weekends, a group of us sixteen-year-olds would go to the beach. Sure, we were looking for girls, but mostly to PARTY, which means get high, drunk, and dabble with some other concoction another kid had in his pocket.

You may wonder how teenagers got beer and liquor?

Shoulder tapping.

A simple, and commonly practiced black-market open system, which operated with immunity back then, and it worked nearly universally.

Two or three of us would hit up different patrons walking into a liquor store with small requests. Did not want them to say no because of one big list, and the fact they would have to carry it all out. One of us would tap a shoulder verbally by saying, "Hey can you pick me up some alcohol?"

"What do you need?"

"A bottle of Jack and a one of Vodka."

As a way of nonverbal acknowledgment in the positive, most would hold out their hand for the cash. Interesting enough the change remained in the bag when they delivered the goods.

Unbelievable.

Others of us would tap a shoulder for beer, receiving a "no" answer to the request happened far less by many multitudes, then the hand out for the cash as the acknowledgement of "sure."

As a teenager I do not remember any of these, go be tweens saying, "be careful, don't drink and drive or don't overdo it." Most of the time we received the hand off with a smile, a nod and "ENJOY."

A different world.

A dangerous place without limitations and an oversupply of perilous opportunities for immature, testosterone infused punk kids. There were a few who died an early unseemly death, but all of us could have ended up as an unconscionable, horrifying statistic, as road kill.

During the summer of my sixteenth year we went to the beach early afternoon and stayed well beyond dark. Designated drivers were years from a common and expected component. None of us even considered the idea. I drove on this occasion. On the way back over the mountain I raced like a complete foolish idiot. Six other kids crammed in with me in the undersized Japanese hatch back. I made it back to the valley without cracking up, but as I sped through a community college parking lot, I allowed my over intoxicated, dimensioned driving ability, to remain hidden behind a false wall of unfounded arrogance and deceit. Next thing I know I went up and over two curbs, clipped a tree, came out the other side spun out and slammed into a brick wall.

A bad crash, but no injuries.

Without prior training, the doors flew open as all the wasted kids took off, darting in all direction. All alone in the dark, I tried to take an inventory and ran off myself. The second crash happened on the strip where all the kids drove back and forth, over and over. Everyone screamed from the side of the road or out open windows as they cruised the strip. Drugs were everywhere and the girls would switch cars at a stop light and were all beautiful, bold and loose.

I slammed into the car in front of me, as my mind and eyes were off the road on other things. No excuse, all my fault. The crash did cause some significant damage to the car I ran into, but did not even leave a scratch on mine. Eight-cylinder engines against a four-piston worm burner, are unequal to the challenge of a low miles per hour fender bender. The doors of both vehicles flung open with scattering adolescences hitting the bushes like terrified squirming rodents who had a bright hot light shined on them. BUSTED, RUN for your LIFE. The driver in the other vehicle fled with the other scaredy heads.

I remained with the accident. I was high this time but not drunk. I did not understand how the protocol worked. Driver's license, insurance? I only knew no one else should receive the blame. I caused the crash I did it and needed to stay and say so.

The first crash I ran. The second I stayed, with no plan, except to face the music reverberation from my reckless actions.

An officer showed up and had me move my car off the road. The kid in the other car left his keys in the ignition so the cop took care of it. Stupid me, I had a freshly used bong in the front seat. I forgot about it.

The officer told me to grab "the paraphilia" from my car. I did. He told me, "empty your pockets." I did, and he took the small bag of weed, shaking his head in disgust and slapping it against the bong in his hand with frustration.

I thought he would take me in.

He looked directly in my eyes and asked, "do you know what this is? I remained silent. "Shit, nothing but shit." He could have taken me in. Marijuana carried significant penalties back then. It would have been a juvenile facility, as I remained under eighteen, but I was clueless. Perfect statement. CLUELESS!

He put the bong under his boot and stomped with a fury and shattered the glass to shreds and swept the shards under a line of hedge bushes. Then he crushed the weed under his heel and turned it to powder.

"I am going to let you go," he told me. I will have the other Yahoo's car towed, serves him right for leaving the scene.

WOW, I thought. Free by the skin of me teeth.

I worked several jobs through my teen years and mostly did well. Pumped gas, worked in a bakery, bagged groceries, things of that nature, but I got fired from a big chain hardware store. Corporate hired a firm to set an elaborate sting operation on many of their employees who worked the cash register. I will not go into the detail of the set up only to say the twenty-dollar bill and one cent laid on the cash register while my line snaked around sat there until no one remained. I put it in my pocket and bingo, busted. They took me upstairs, tongue thrashed me, fired me and set me packing, making my name mud. Worse than mud. I got the job on the recommendation of an older girl in our wide and broad circle who took my indiscretion personal. She, as a manager, the one who vouched for me, spread the slanted details of my crime across our community of pot smoking teenagers. So, not only was I a burn-out, drop-out, looser, I became a thief to boot. Oh, the glories of childhood. The gossip spread far wide and at lightning speed. I became anathema, so I did not look for a job, sat around and did nothing, going nowhere with no prospects. Then my father started a new business in the State Capital of Sacramento. He wanted me to move with him, for a new start, while the rest of the family, those who still remained living in the house, waited until the house sold.

Interesting enough, the manager who helped me get the job, fell under the spell of the corporate sting operation and got canned. I do not remember any of the gossip hounds reaching out to me to take back the venomous gossip they heard and spread.

Bless them.

I turned into an adult in Sacramento. Or I should say, I turned eighteen. I did not know what my father did exactly, but he had a well thought out plan for me.

Education and a job.

He helped me enroll in the community college and look for a job. I did my best to listen and study, but it became very clear, very quick, I naturally lacked the aptitude for school. I am not sure why I never told my father my struggles with class room-based education, but as we lived outside the big city together, alone, I opened up. He understood somehow.

"God gave you gifts, and I have no doubt you will succeed in a big way. A very big way. School is just not for you. Don't worry about it."

I believe with no question; my DAD is the greatest man who ever lived. Plain and simple.

An underserved gift I can never repay.

While we lived together, he taught me to golf, and we played many rounds. I handed down his set of clubs to one of the seven recently. We played tennis together, went to the arcade, he liked the old game PAC-MAN, I like Asteroid's. We lived in a small furnished, kind of crappy, apartment, but I loved it and still cherish the time we shared so many decades ago which for some unexplainable reason feels as if they were lived only yesterday.

One of the wonders of life.

My days of struggle and trouble were not over. I realize now, they never are for anyone, but I have come to see, it is what we do with the curve balls coming over the plates of our lives that produce fruit either sweet or rotten. Swinging with selfishness, bitterness, anger, blame, produce a poisonous, toxic cesspool internally and destruction externally all around.

I found out the hard way.

I found a job as a telemarketer and achieved limited success and moved up. An odd job, calling strangers and pitching products over the phone, but I found an ability to not antagonize while still asking for the sale.

"I appreciate that, have you ever considered, would it make a difference," were some techniques taught, and I used them without making prospective customers on the line angry. "Ask for the sale three times, then be polite and move on." Sure, people slammed the phone on me, but another training tip in the arsenal of telemarketing stated, "better to find out they are rude up front so they do not waste your time."

It is a law of numbers.

As I succeeded making problematic sales, I failed in my personal life. Amazing how in a strange city, not knowing anyone, you can hook up with the sort you seemed to know all your life. The partiers, the druggies, with wide connections. In no time, I connected with a broad diverse group spread around several jurisdictions. "ADULTS hosted the parties" from the State college called "Frat Parties."

Not a weekend without one and there seemed to be competing parties, as if they were being rated on some unseen balancing scale, so we raced from house to house, not sure why, I guess to find the best one.

Late, after midnight, driving alone I followed a couple other cars to the next big one, better one and missed a turn, so I flipped a U-turn and bingo, flashing lights.

Busted.

They administered three tests. Walk the line, touch your nose, say the alphabet backwards. Failed, failed, failed. Drunk Driving. DUI. Mothers Against Drunk Drivers, MADD, arrived with a vengeance, and rightly so, they need a commendation for their diligence and tenacity. What a sad fact and I am the worst of the worst. I could have killed someone, maybe one of their kids.

Horrible.

My car got impounded, and I got incarcerated. The beginning of a life change.

After a day, they cut me loose, with a time to appear in court six month away, suspended driver's license and a fine with a jail sentence lingering out in the distance. I deserved it.

The straight sentence for a first offense of drunk driving held an unapologetic six-months behind bars. No bargains. Six months in county jail.

Crap.

I spent time in county jail before and held no interest in returning. While in Sacramento, before the DUI, my father needed to travel for business for a couple weeks, instead of staying by myself, in the furnished apartment, I went back home for a mini vacation. It did not turn out well. I hooked up with the wrong group who turned the age of accountability without wisdom.

A hit of Acid, snorts of who knows what, bong hits, tokes on a cocaine freebase pipe, left me reeling, untethered and completely tweaked. I easily could have died by ways of an overdose, instead they took me in, booked me and threw me in the slammer. By the time I came down, I received the negative response my mother had no intention of getting me out. "Keep him in there and let him learn his lesson." Not a bad call as I look back. At the time I wanted to blow my stack and fly off the handle. Instead, I let loose with childish belligerence and the unjustified anger of a punk.

The night of my DUI, I blew into a plastic tube which quantifies the amount of alcohol in your blood stream. 1.0 and you are drunk. Six months in county period. I blew .09, and they gave me a reckless driving instead. No jail time, a larger fine, my driver's license back with restriction for seven years.

Skin of my teeth.

Not too long after I received my right to drive again, a car slammed in to the back of my car leaving me without wheels and a need to stick my thumb out hitching rides to and from work. As I mentioned earlier, A guy I worked with in the telephone sales gig, picked me up, shared the unpolluted gospel of grace, through the Lord Jesus Christ and WAM, a one-step program. No more smoking, drinking, doing drugs or going with girls who do. Like a light switch going off, I became a new creature.

A powerful transformation.

For a couple of years, I floated on cloud nine of the goodness of God. I got a great job at a large telecommunications firm working in their mammoth computer room. Microfiche Specialist, Tape Operator, Printing Specialists were the titles. All those jobs are extinct now as a watch on your wrist or sleek glass screen in your back pocket hold more power by several multitudes than the CPU's in the big air-conditioned rooms back then. Amazing. I loved the job and the people and I found a degree of success, although I did not fit in the inner circle as my speech went to the side of polite and tempered and I did not get drunk, smoke dope or party anymore. I did not preach, condemn or act superior, but they did not invite me to the after-hours get togethers. I do not blame them, plus I spent time with a large group at church from a wide variety of backgrounds all coming into agreement with the simple message.

The Lamb of God takes away the sins of the world.

Outstanding.

Then Out of the Blue, crippling depression pounded me into the dirt, leaving me dysfunctional, reeling, flailing, in despair.

From there, as I explained, I polluted myself with far reaching doctrinal and religious philosophy, manic living, information overload, dreaming up wild ideas with a hope to produce revenue instead of failure, I bought stuff, poured out my self-focused cockamamie opinions, until the curtain I stood behind got torn to shreds leaving me mentally naked and exposed.

A rambling road filled with many pot holes, detours and dead ends, but gave me the most important gift.

THE BEAUTIFUL PERFECT SEVEN. All beautiful, all perfect without question. Greater than great, better than Amazing, Outstanding, Fabulous, Incredible.

Perfect.

The most important work GOD ever did, from across all the cosmos, is the design, creation of the Beautiful Perfect Seven.

It is an undisputable fact, hands down.

When you live with an overload of religious indoctrination, from sea to shining sea, and the culture around you makes stratospheric adjustments every few years, it would be abuse to continue the probation I established against the evils of the world. You knew the bad stuff out there. The Seven came into my care from no ability of my own and I owed it to them to make sure they had a fighting chance in the future world they would exist in. I had to adjust for the sake of my children. They grew in a world quaking with high velocity tectonic shifts and no one could say where things would end up except everyone knew there is no going back. Going from analog to a hyper super-duper-zipping digital world with very few manuals to study, time to decide, came with more than a few stumbling blocks. I did not care. I made a crystal-clear decision, which went against judgement, condemnation and downright vile opinions from the upright and uptight religious zealots, most were mothers as their husbands cowered under the thumb of their godly wives. A seriously sad reality, but true. It did not matter to me. My name had been mud more times than I can count, plus, none of those pious bitties would be there if one of the Seven struggled with thoughts of suicide, sexual orientation, fear, anxiety, so I did not only shift, I tilted all in, for the sake of my beautiful wonderful children. They did not choose to be born at this time, in this exceptional new world, and how dare I put a probation on them from the technology they would have to understand and find their way. Texting is a new language I use, but they live on. They do not call customer service when an issue arises, they go online and take care of it. I still write checks, put a stamp on an envelope and send it through the mail. They do not even carry currency. I feel naked if I do not have cash in my pocket. I use debit and credit cards most of the time, but having dollar bills with me gives me a degree of comfort, not the Beautiful Seven. They are a cashless society.

Got to love the new world.

I understood my children would become adults in a strange new land and it seemed to me, new languages, connections, technology would become part of their daily life and future existence. I held no keys to see the future, I did not even see the new language would come in the form of texts or friendships would come from distance places, but it did not matter. I did not need to know, I could see, times and technology were changing and my children should not, could not, stand and exist as ignorant outsiders. As a confession, I purposely created a path, when the first few were itty-bitty little ones, to exist in a sequestered life, I knew I needed to act and fast. As I look back, I refer to my shallow, fear-based philosophy of child rearing as, THE AMISH PATH, which is exactly the path they were on based on my weakness to listen and follow the road of protective blinders so they would not see the big bad world out there. It is very big and extremely bad, and what father would not want to protect his beloved offspring from the wiles of the uncharted, lightning fast, wide open world with multitudes of unhealthy voices shouting to the wind with temptation and finger rolling seduction?

What is a biased father to do?

Have faith in my children and do all I could to help them navigate the dark tributaries and make sure they had a refuge they could count on.

The cultural world has always changed. Most alterations came with strutters and spirts, but in the end real quantifiable progress took place. New inventions, a better way to do things, less expensive widely distributed products, a sweet new widget is part of the historical human experience going back centuries. Railroad over a stage coach, automobiles over horse and buggy, Freon based cooling systems over an ice box. Many changes have come and gone with fantastic long-term beneficial outcomes overall, but at the time of change from analog to the fast-moving charts of digital and wireless does not come with a step-by-step transition or a diagram to dip a toe into the rushing stream of treacherous rapids and skull bashing boulders of information.

Plug and Play became the new instructional manual. Tap it and take a ride on the highway of uncontainable information and then the APPS came. Free apps. Download till your hearts content. The variety seems uncountable or quantifiable.

Golly GEE.

It felt to me, just a little guy, as an endless playground for the future debt ridden to get a start. Vendors, advertisers, charlatans, propaganda peddlers who needed eye balls to get their rocks off and rack in revenue by the truck load and I said yes and AMEN to the most beautiful perfect seven to take a ride on the super highway. I do not look back with regret, other than I would have taken more time to highlight some ditches, crack and stomping blocks. I tried, but I am another generation, an old generation, so I treaded with care. I trust the magic in my children and guard against going down the rabbit hole of the peddlers and con artists.

It is amazing we have so little ability to see the future at the time of beginnings of significant transition in a new industry or technology. I do not have the luxury to look back and make changes or alterations, so I trust. Too much change came out of nowhere, back there, flinging at high speed into my head and before my children's eyes, to contemplate, equate, or evaluate, so I went all in, with a degree of caution, preparation and a great deal of investigation.

The powerful shift and bright shining options came from nowhere out of every direction, fast and clear with tempting allure, month by month. Not over decades or years, it felt as if day by day. An onslaught of mostly, Mr. Rogers approved free downloadable applications at first. Games, plenty of bright colored games, then came many concerning issues which do not have historical precedent as the change held no compass to compare. From the early nineteen nineties until the first half decade of the new millennium the perfect seven went from pre-internet, to every pocket holding all information from before time, available with only a swipe or thumbs up.

I personally paid and gave each of the Seven a device and also paid for the upgrades on purpose.

Yes, yes, yes. Upgrade, more, more, better.

On purpose.

I chose to give each of my children the latest shiny devices with an open mind and clear conscious. To this day, I have no interest in social media. I do not need thumbs to turned up and I do not feel comfortable with the platforms of shallow declarations. I hold no honor in this decision nor do I care. I like what I like and multitudes like other things, I get it, but God only gave the seven into my care so I focus on them and their place in this world.

Sorry, if you have authority over something else, please feel free to do as you will. I will say that is the greatest thing God is doing on the earth in your life and I will be the first to stand back, bow down, salute and pray for you.

May your focus remain stable.

I only have the Seven. They are my priority. Even if they do not need me.

Many stood in my path, but I side stepped most of them. I put my head down with both hands holding firm to my unusual conviction against the judgmental grain with one purpose. Make sure my children had the best opportunity to take the greatest foot forward so they could become the best in this life. I should throw out a secret. I prayed for them day and night as I believe THE HOLY SPIRIT moves with hidden power for a specific purpose. It does not mean things are easy.

The task became arduous but I held firm against the fear-based condemnation crowd.

Bless their tiny self-focused fearful hearts.

I made a specific choice to school the Seven at home. I understand this may seem odd and a bit cooky, but I did it anyway with conviction. The county school would take any of them in at a moment's notice and lick their chops for the annual funding from the big bad powerful "STATE."

Revenue.

Dollars for kids, what a sad and disgusting fact. Welcome to the way of the public-school system. Everyone knows it, but no one will address the monster in the room. Been this way since way back when...

Fill in your own blanks.

How many blanks are there?

Too many to fill in.

I took out a loan called, A TAKEOUT LOAN, to build a house on a scrap of dirt in the country and don't ya know, they gave me a tax bill for the school districts my children would not attend. No problem, just part of life. It made me think about the old folks who, (had no kids but built a house) needed to pay taxes on their new construction, but I had kids, a bunch of kids, I could have unloaded on the super sacrificial servants of the State who only want to serve the tiny heads of mush with social indoctrination more than the three "R's."

With eyes wide opened, and arms spread to the horizon, a slight cold heart, and a disabled blind eye, I made the CHOICE to school my offspring at home instead of the clear choice to abdicate their "SCHOOLING" to divided educators. You know, the union, the management, the State and the REGULATORS.

Aren't they the ones who you want to give all your investments to manage? Give them your children instead.

Most do, without question.

Call me PRO-CHOICE. I made the choice with clear conviction and a sober understanding.

I heard, and still hear, all the less than well thought out philosophies about socialization, need for interaction, and all the other shit, but trust me, I did not make this decision without thought.

The real and clear problem with HOME SCHOOLING is the group of people it gathers around you. I have taken time to consider, and it took me more time than I want to express, to come into the one true, specific, illustrative conclusion I will convey as my best proper description.

Christian homeschooling is a fear based, proud, finger pointing, weak, deceptive, female driven CULT.

I also understand my definition may seem a bit off the cuff or slightly off handed, but it is the best I can do and it is very accurate.

How sad.

I came to the place where I realized, all seven needed to be able to READ anything they wanted to at Any Time, Any Place, as well as write all they thought up, and cipher anything they needed to. READ, WRITE and CYPHER. Interfacing with the wider world around them became an important part of education I believed, as the world started to spin faster with new technology and massive amounts of input, and the cloistered living I allowed and bowed to, would not serve them well. In fact, it would make them disabled and cause suffering. One day, not in the too distant future, they held no choice but to leave and go into a world the homeschool agenda could never prepare them for, so I pivoted significantly.

This did not go over well with the afraid, pious, finger pointing crowd.

Movies, Video games, and Cell phones.

By the time the first four of the Seven started to transition from happy, sweet, innocent kids, to beautiful real people with clear distinct personalities and thoughts of their own, I made a conscious choice to completely shift and do my best to prepare them for the world they had no choice but to live in. I threw out literature, they could read to their hearts desire the classics at their own leisure some time down the road. Time became of the ESSENCE, with deep urgency in me. I needed to make up ground and fast for their sake. For some odd reason I found myself persuaded years before to see the devil in just about everything and I take the blame. Cinderella had magic, BAD, Power Rangers shows demons, OFF LIMITS, Pokémon CAST SPELLS, Harry Potter is a wizard, OH the HORROR. I shut the first four of the perfect Seven out from the basic understanding of this wild, flying culture, out of Fear. I listened to the worries of others and acted accordingly.

No more I decided. No more for their sake.

Trust God? Or cover your children's eyes.

I chose to take the blinders off and TRUST.

I hold a deep regret for my weakness. Allowing others to guide MY path is one thing, but not for…

The Beautiful Perfect Seven!

They deserved, needed better and certainly merited the promise to have some preparation for the world they would enter and take over, so I made specific decisions, choices, regarding the input and interaction of the broader culture. I chose to have them watch all sorts of movies. The classic Disney movies, Warner Bros cartoons, MGM classics, Rogers & Hammerstein musicals and just about every cultural significant movie out there. I did not restrict ratings. An "R" did not become an issue to me. The value of the story held a higher value. This is back in the day of video tapes in brick and mortar bright and colorful, VIDEO STORES. They do not exist anymore, but back then, the options bulged and I took full advantage. Rent five for a buck apiece and get five children's movies for free.

The good old days.

My choice of education, given from the collaborative works of very dedicated and talented film makers, over decades, did not go over well with the finger pointing condemners. I did not care. I pitied them and they judged me. They did not have the best interest of my children in the forefront of their thoughts, and they held zero responsibility or authority for the upbringing of the Seven or their souls.

A wide range of movies became a staple, or more like a feast, and the fruit did not make my children, callused, greedy, worldly, cruel. On the contrary, nearly every story holds profound messages I could never, in the life of me convey, but went deep into them with value in their lives to this day.

Overcoming, self-sacrifice, generosity, love, to name a few.

I can still see, in my mind's eye, and hear in a comforting place of remembrance, the popcorn bowls spilled across the carpet, the tiny people in their PJ's, laughing, crying, or feeling a bit afraid. Many of the best conversation I have had with the Seven come from stories piped through a device, hooked to a tube, pouring out fantastic music, brilliant cinematography and heart moving dialog.

I made the choice and I should have done it sooner.

Video Games.

The first two of the Seven became enamored with video games at an early age. It feels like centuries ago, but it is only two decades. Technology back then started to increase with some burps and starts but in the end, it took hold and I saw the Writing on the Wall. There were wide swaths of devices and games. I went all in. Let them play their brains out became my mantra, and I believed it wholeheartedly.

I witnessed several of the older kids in the homeschooling community who had suffered under a prohibition on video games who went off the deep end when they became adults and left home. If that is not clear writing on the Wall, I do not know what is. The young who became adults, denied a recreation needing to overdo the indulgence when they should be getting on with life. I wanted my children to experience many of these issues while they still remained under my roof, where I might still have some value to instill wisdom and insight. I did not want them to get it from the, "Yahoos" out there. No subject became taboo, and I gave my best.

With some regret, or maybe many regrets, many of my words were leavened with dogma, twinges of fear, and as I said before, "My Own Haughty Misguided Opinion," but in the end they opened up wide and many times I would just give the facts about a word they heard, or confusing cultural phrase. Interesting enough I am the one asking things I do not know about out there in the new world. They have proven to be patient with my old guy cultural ignorance.

Cell Phones.

The biggest choice, which went against the grain of bony finger pointing accusers, has to be my purposeful purchase of thin glass screen devices everyone now holds in their pockets and pull out like they are sucking their thumbs. I went to an airport and waited for a flight and left my thumb sucking device in my pocket and observed all those around me. Try it some time. WOW. The facial expressions are awesome to witness as they swipe, type, smile, frown.

Holy cow.

That is an incongruent statement. Cows are not Holy.

Anyhow, I gave all seven the shiny devices. They have since grown beyond my knowledge and I find myself in need of instruction. They treat me well in my ignorance in my slow as a slug tendency.

I told you.

They are the Beautiful Perfect Seven.

Since then I have come to a profound but unsettling revelation. I am one of the old ones now. Their time arrived and I have hope for their future. I hear people putting down these new generations with lame sound bites filled with unfounded judgement. I have heard these same statements made by the generation before mine, so I take it with a grain of salt.

I chose to be hopeful and optimistic about the exceptional generations behind mine. After all, they will have to pay all the bills which surely will come do.

How wrong are the BOOMER's? Selfish, proud, short sighted.

I am one from the old days now. I always thought my parents and grandparents came from that ethereal place, then I realized the beautiful seven are able to tell stories of life before the internet, flip phones, VHS movies, Blockbuster. Days before streaming, before WIFI. When texting only came through nine plus zero on a keypad on the bottom side of the flip phone. To spell words, you pushed a button several times until you reach the right letter. One thumb push gave you an "A". Two more a "C". A new language, a wonderful language and a language left in the dust pile of extinction within several years. Half of the seven will be able to tell this tale. They have others to tell. The way of the world.

The circle of life.

With the incarnation and arrival of the glass screens, created in the mind of a genius, would go on to change the whole wide world before he died from a disease technology could have treated. Maybe those days are behind us and we will all live forever. Not outside the scope nowadays. Interesting, the GENIUS who thought up, pushed through and change the world with hand held magic devices, chose natural treatment to shrink tumors and disease instead of cutting it out and pounding it with FDA approved poison. But I digress. A change took place. A generational shift with unprecedented upward and amazing results. A worldwide cultural shift with technology beyond imagination. Everything you needed in your pocket. Shiny, sleek, brilliant. Pinch, swish, tap and type. Internet, phone, maps, instant message with a full keyboard, no more need to use a keypad to share your thoughts or communicate. Google, Samsung, Apple and Microsoft were in the nowhere land of the future to copy new technology as competition and profit. The app store did not exist except in the vision of where version two would go.

What could be better? Dinner with friends, a quiet walk on the beach, reading a book by the fireplace, taking a long restful nap, reminiscing with old friends are a few, but shiver my timbers, the glass master connected devices regulates most of true pleasures in the back seat, under a dusty pillow, forgotten and disregarded. No one cared, the entire world lives in a pocket. Two fingers pull it out and a single thumb swipe brings it to life with more information than could ever be fully digested from a bright little screen.

Great and amazing. So cool. A life changer.

On that day I knew the Seven needed to have the glass phones in their pockets, otherwise they would be behind the curve in a world they were ignorant of. A world changing by the moment. Hellfire came against me from the small-minded hypocrites. I think I spent a decade hearing second hand whispers of gossip against me, but my heart and mind only tilted to the Seven. They were the only ones given to me where I held true responsibility. They were my main concern in a drastic changing world and I took my responsibility serious. I did not want them to be incapable, so I thrust into their young hands the high-priced product with all the world at their fingertips. High definition pornography, hate speak, false doctrine, mindless media, gossip and worthless philosophies. With a sober mind I chose to give the Seven a gift which could destroy them. But as I said the Seven are beautiful and perfect. I whole heartily believed even though some were very young, small and needing years of experience to decipher and decide. I did not have the time, so I went all in against many loud, angry, accusing voices. I knew those aggressive voices lived in weakness behind a predetermined mindset based on works-based purity and fear.

I struggled with the new language of texting, I still do, but I did not need to be an instructor. The schooling of the language came free of charge and I cheered them all on to find their own sweet spot. I opened up my device to the social network craze only to understand and give some guidance to my children. They learned fast and I trust them. On the other hand, I did not personally find an interest in "thumbs up, tweets and likes," so I fired big tech for myself, and buried my social footprint.

We each like what we like. Choose as you will.

I understood there are many life skills which need instruction and training and I am the first to say I failed in many areas, big time, but isn't it interesting how rare those important parts of life seem to come into daily life?

Technology moves at lightning fast speed and my imagination can only wonder, which is unhealthy for me, so I trust and do not complain. I told most of the Seven, "one day there will not be a screen or device, it will be holographic colors you touch in floating spaces everywhere."

I could not help myself.

Switching gears.

That part of my therapeutic journey brought with it a sweet comfort walking down memory lane with The Seven at the core.

Getting on track, back to the issues at hand.

I am currently in an uneasy place, months removed from the point when my mind seemed to come unglued with a terrify detachment from reality. I am by no means all the way to where

I want to be, desire, understand and know I need to be, but I am on a path, in a trajectory, in the direction to possible stability and balance. It has been a bumpy isolated road with many switch backs and deadly potholes. I have been pushed down, stymied and deceived from forces I never met before while I press on with a dry diligent heart toward a goal which elutes me.

I pivoted and bobbed, twisted, backed up, questioned, drew context, turned around all in a white-knuckle grip of determination both from natural instinct and spiritual possibility and have learned a few things. Embryotic things, with real power and a genuine prospect in the direction of stability, normality and balance.

Episodes.

Most days now, I feel fine and perfectly normal, if there is such a thing. Tears still come out of the Blue and buzzing anxiety has a way with me but all in all, I have come back from the brink, for the most part, but not all the way. Maybe I never fully will. I have learned, am learning, from nowhere at any time, a flare up, based on certain triggers can show its ugly head before me with gripping sharp claws making an undesired request to have its will with me while I struggle not to fall into a trap and find myself stuck in an unmovable quagmire fighting alone in a hellish internal battle with horrible uncomfortable physical feelings with real-world implications. Frustration, anger, buzzing apprehension, terror, fidgety twitches and contortions in my facial expression.

I stand guard, aware and prepared so things do not go too far off the rail. I am learning and am aware at a moment's notice deep or shallow emotional instability can play me like a disregarded out of tune fiddle and I can fall into an unhealthy, unwelcome pit.

A terrible place I cannot expect to go away. I have no choice except to learn, stand aware, practice and fight.

Some of these episodes are small, simple blips and I can find my footing without too much difficulty and come back to a stable stance and clear thought in no time. Others are horrible, unexplainable, treacherous, evil, tricky, holding my face in the muck with the rest of me floundering in painful defeat.

No one else knows unless I bring it to the light. Unless I freak out with crazy talk or bouncing frustration which does nothing but hurt others, so I still hide. This all happens down inside me, unheard by others, invisible but so difficult.

Real but unseen.

Fighting an unseen enemy inside my head.

This is a tangible problem I am working to understand and combat with less than satisfactory results. At a moments notice, I recognize, I am susceptible to many unruly emotions for no reason and completely unacceptable in polite society. Actually, unacceptable anywhere, in any place, at any time.

Triggers.

I am learning there are many triggers I need to see coming, recognize the intend, and allow to move by with the least amount of thought as possible, either through avoidance or disinterest as they hold unbalanced power against me. One day, in a place of balance, stability, and longevity, I hope to be able to bypass any of these triggers and smile with gratitude at how small and powerless they are and have always been. Until that sweet day, I am on guard with a fairly confident anticipation these are no more than small flies on the wall or tiny little gnat's in the wind.

A worthy endeavor in hope.

There are more than three places I can find myself tripped up, stumbling and caught in a decrepit net of emotional upheaval and confusion but I will highlight three.

Opinions. No one hears. Difficulties.

This could be a Ramble but I am choosing to get it out.

It may seem hypocritical to make accusation against others for their opinions as I confessed my dark tendency toward using my opinion as a weapon. No one else needs to hold back their own thoughts or beliefs with verbal expression or through art, music or in written form. I have no qualms with anyone expressing their views whenever and however they wish. The struggle is in me. I am aware my mind can spark and ignite and blast off at the smallest, benign unimportant statement or a great big and sweeping expression as an opinion from, political thought, religious conviction and a seemly endless list. Child rearing, over general negative statements about whole groups of people as a generation, culture or race, sexual ordination, death penalty, abortion, fossil fuels, technology, the list can go on and on. Any and all of these opinions need open free discussion and debate, but each have the possibility to become an unhealthy trigger for me with consequences of treachery left in the wake. I need to learn, am learning, not to engage, able to listen with no Topsy Turvy side effects. Tweaked screwed up episodes.

I have been practicing with some favorable results.

Some.

Opinions out of nowhere from wide polar opposite places at any time, need to not affect me negatively, but they do, so mostly, I side step, and avoid, get away. My goal is to be able to listen and hear and accept any philosophy or opinion not matter how well thought out or how shallow they may come across my plate.

I need time and practice to perfect a place of not blasting off into a spinning episode down a road to emotional upheaval.

This is my weakness, mine alone, so I will need to stand guard with vigilance.

Small, not well thought out statements coming from corrupt seeds of a biased place based on narrow thoughts, bug the shit out of me, and they should not have the power to take me out, but if I ponder and play with the worthless pride centered, ignorant, shallow statements, watch out.

Not a good sight to see or hear.

In the political realm it is somewhat understandable. I will never have a conversation with the endless supply of head talking pundits so I have learned to turn them off for the most part. I dabble but that is my choice and part of my therapy. These paid talkers have every right to spout out phrases which might have gone through the cleaners and washed by focused groups. Both sides do this and I have little difficulty accepting the game, the scam, the reason. Both sides want to get the ball over the goal line and say we WON. They didn't. The founders with quill pens created unmovable stumbling blocks so the winners of the MAJORITY cannot stomp on the faces of the MINORITY, sorry, just the way of the rules came out.

But the winners can take the flimsy reigns in a small victory lap and then suffer the consequences of their haughty, conviction driven side of the isle the minority hates. The tides turn every few years. Winners whine like losers and do their best to use the rules to stand as a counterweight to the newly crowned majority. In the end they will lose power in two or four years, been that way from way back when.

Not sure why these overheated hypocrites continue to blather on.

Just a fact and a truth. Those who win or lose their power after they fight for their own small-minded agenda and win only find themselves in the back seat of the minority, where real power sits. Sixty percent, or two thirds to overturn.

A brilliant guard rail and huge speed bump, woven into the fabric of the hand written, founding, two-page scrolled document.

The Constitution of the United States of America, plus the ten amendments, stick like welded stones as a real problematic boulder against these politicians, despots, dictators, bleeding heart hypocrites and all the rest of the well-meaning, self-promoting, sick-a-pants, deceptively working to have their way, but the rules established two centuries before, keep them impotent and grasping for a single cell to impregnate, or abort.

Take your pick.

So sad. So pitiful, and so horrifying. These reprobates will do anything to get their agenda through and they do have power, but LET NOT YOUR HEART BE TROUBLED, they might find a way only to see themselves eating their own words.

Technology is a powerful resource.

Play it back.

When they, either they or them, get the super majority, you know two thirds, they will all be benevolent to the minority, the ones who have different opinions but are fewer in number than the rulers, YOU SHALL NOT disagree with.

God forbid you disagree.

They might lock you up. Hung. Crucified. Tarred and feathered.

Pick any other you came conquer up.

Progressive or Conservative, they have all proven for decades they will pound and cancel the DESENTERS. God bless you if you open your mouth against the ONES in Control, but watch out and look for cover.

Sad if you are on the wrong side of the isle. Wait and it will shift in a favorable direction or one far worse and more horrifying, but it might come back with the pendulum swinging in your favor, but I would not count on it. Seems to me the stop watch is ticking faster. TIMES they are a CHANGIN. Maybe a financially bankrupt world will bring things back inline. GLOBAL meltdown. Not recession or depression, but a complete meltdown. A real true genuine shaking of the world.

Reset the clock.

I am only pondering.

How fantastic to look back and see the FATHER's, the thinkers fight through a spanking brand-new nation against the unfeeling IMPERIALIST king many leagues away.

The slave owners, the deists, the puritan Christians, and the honest convicted patriots, individual rights, land owners, simple people from thirteen different colonies with massive diverse thoughts, beliefs and interests and sophisticated OPINIONS gathered together to pound out a DECLARATION, declaring independence. Then a constitution where some human beings are only three fifths of a person.

Two thirds to change. Sixty percent to pass a law, out of the senate, majority out of the house, so the out of control executive branch cannot usurp the rights of free human beings, peoples, individuals.

This give and take happened for many decades in the federal system, but seems not be alive and well today. I could be wrong, I have been many, many times.

In some States, SUPER MAJORITies reign with unchecked power. Watch out they might bulldoze the minority party with wide smiles on their faces. These rulers, these makers of laws could become unhinged and one day the Tick Tock teens will grow up and rebuke them all to the max.

But these rulers, who believe with their whole inexpert hearts, will cheat and do their darndest to change the rules. But it takes sixty percent in the Senate to send a bill out for the floor vote at least it used to be. Nowadays it looks like a simple majority will do the trick.

The scoundrels who give allegiance to party over personal conviction, religious opinions, information based talking points spray out with inept empty voices to the wind proving they are blind guides.

Political and hypocritical.

Watching too much, brings me to my knees.

Sorry a bit of a repetitive ramble there.

Switching gears back.

Seeing the faces of people, studying their eyes, the movement around their cheeks, their eyebrows, even the shape of their noses when they talk and express themselves with animation, anger, sorrow, pride, hope, excitement and an endless supply of other emotions, makes my guts bounce, with a weakness in my ankles and increased flow in my blood stream.

I have found many blinking lights, leading the way from diverse places and have concluded on the slip and slide of life, twists and turns come from nowhere. There are days when I truly believe I am all the way back, but I understand this is a dangerous illusion with dire consequences.

I need to hear and see all opinions without spinning out like I just did.

Hear, listen and smile.

People could not hear me.

I came to see, through many interactions and a degree of experimental observation, numerous people could not, or chose not, to hear me. It might have been their minds where elsewhere, or they were thinking ahead and missed my clear, defined words. I am not talking about hearing or grasping large conversations, those seemed to flow and have an impact with confirmation in the two way give and take, but giving one liners, or unmistakable statements, I would speak out with unbroken clarity for some odd and strange reason could not be heardf and went overlooked even though there is no way to misunderstand the context.

I like lime soda.

Interest rates need to go up, but then the house of cards will crumble to dust.

This next generation is better than us.

Bitterness and blame hurt you not the ones you hate, SORRY.

I find more contentment in self-denial than in the false glitters many worship.

Pay more for a car and brag how you gave the best deal to the dealer and the salesperson who helped you get your hands around such a great and marvelous new vehicle. Boast on the deal they got, not on how you fought to nickel and dime them down.

I could give others, but I made the point.

At no time did anyone engage. It seems to me they just went blank, so I learned to check such statements or declarations.

A very odd and weird part of life for me.

I spoke with simple clarity. I did not have an ulterior motive, except the one giving the car dealer a better deal, what can I say, but the others and so many more fell on deaf ears. They still do. It is an issue I am working to overcome, or get out from under as I move forward.

For some unknown reason, over my life, I would not or could not be heard. In more times than I can count, although for some reason I did not even consider the oddity on people's faces as their expressions turned off and went blank. A fact I lived with. Now, I not only consider, but I am working like a data driven scientist to uncover the reason and purpose so I do not fall into a ditch I am unable to escape from. I hold my tongue and watch my words until such a day I hope will come.

People who cannot or do not hear me is not the issue. My mind and thoughts are. Bless all others as I guard, watch and hold my words in reserves.

Difficulties.

I can sense the beginning of a rumble and the propensity to ramble on my part, when I engage in a conversation on certain subjects. It starts slow with a slight buzzing in my chest until it sends electric currents pulsating through my whole-body building to frustration making my speech stutter and tremble as it raises to a fevered pitch. Within no time, confusion enters and I find myself in a verbal quagmire. This is a significant difficulty and one I need to get a hold of, wrestle and pin to the mat in some semblance of victory.

Rambles and an Issue.

I am going to take a time of indulgence to illustrate how my mind works. I look for a permissive place of grace and a bit of openness as I take a turn and go on a hidden path toward instability in hopes it may serve as an illustration with value. A few play by plays, I will lay out, as a demonstration, of how I justify or argue on a specific subject.

I have spent countless hours and worthless back and forth on many subjects. I will try to type and tap out on a keyboard to give a picture of my wondering mind.

These come to me fully intact, in a matter of seconds, and I am working to let them die on the vine, go dormant so I might see and live in the light of day away from torment.

I am still unable to prefect the method, but I am trying.

Sometimes the ramble twists down unconnected alleys which give me an opportunity to take a different off ramp and end at a foreign place from where I intended to arrive, while at other times I end exactly where I set out with a complete thought.

A Rambling thought.

There will be some redundancy here as I understand through my time of this written talk therapy, I keep coming back to a theme so hang with me.

I have held back from going to the end verbally in conversations with people as it has not proven to be of value. What better place, than written talk therapy, to go full bore. I will illustrate two rambles and one issue focused event I witnessed out of the hundreds of wildcat curving slow balls of whacked out thoughts and one recent issue infiltrating my head and heart. Not sure where this will end, or the value, I only feel compelled to give it a shot, roll the dice and open up. It seems clear it will be up to others to make the choice. Put me down, diagnosis from the stained arm chair of your couch or by all means get riled up and make highbrow accusations against me. Why should I care and what good would it do?

Cancel me. Cancel me. Cancel me.

We have become the sweet cancel culture. Am I wrong, who can say, but I shine the tiny beam of light in the new world of tweets, uploads, downloads, thumbs up or down, THAT IS BAD INCASE YOU DID NOT KNOW? Down thumbs are BAD. Go to the front of the class and pull out a box of chalk and write on the board one hundred times you dunce, you dunce, you dunce until sophisticated society undoes the CANCEL on you. Grab your knees, bend over and beg.

It is after all a new part of our shared culture.

Here goes RAMBLE one.

Just like the governmental, pompous cowards and hypocrites. You know the shallow law makers, on both sides of the isles, who did not even pass the smallest basic written laws to make a different for the masses under the heavy arm of regulatory STAY AT HOME orders. History should hold those accused with guilty verdicts and with welts on their deceiving knuckles, but I digress, let's be clear, most will all get reelected in a landslide. Please forgive me for a useless indulgence in fantasy.

In the end the truth shines in painful and brutal clear reflection. The political prostitutes will continue to slither out of the muck, grow and rise up with proud boastful abdication to the Big "E" executives who used a pen and phone to sign, what do they call it? "EXECUTIVE ORDERs" for the unionized lifelong city, county, state and federal employees to act as ENFORCERS to seek out, find and fine and, on the other hand maybe imprison violators of their scribbled whims of fancy. What happened to the law makers? How are new regulations enforceable laws? But let's get real, incarceration is on the back burner. The executives have taken over as quasi law makers, issuing orders, with ambiguous unenforceable regulations over the old school. You know actual debated, passed and sign in laws. The old square share, sometimes corrupt but fought out, passed and then signed into an actual law placed on the books, challenged in the courts to confirm if, THE LAWS, are in line with the original, or tradition, or precedent, of the law itself and THE CONSTITUTION.

I guess that is a perfect illustration of original intent or should we go by precedence.

Are executive orders constitutional? A fair question in this new and challenging world when the executive has a pen, a phone, a mega phone, thousands of government paid employees under them, many with guns and so much more. It used to be the executive could use their authority to buy flowers or plates for the white house or governor's mansion, but now the Executive branch is the one over the most government paid employees and departments. The second branch under the constitution, The Executive branch, THE ENFORCERS, is huge. Massive. Bigger than big. They make the, first branch, The Legislative, THE MAKERS, and the third branch, the Judicial, THE INTERPETERS, look like famine-stricken refugees.

It only costs six billion green backs yearly to feed and clothe, THE FIRST BRANCH, and only twenty-five billion for the Judicial branch. How much for the enforcers? Hard to say. The Executive branch has nearly uncountable departments. The tree tilts, ready to fall over and uproot. The appointed run the ship as temporary employees called SECRETARIES over department such as the State Department and the Department of Defense, that means the branches of the military and the great complex keeping them supplied with toilet paper and laser-guided missiles. How many other departments, sub departments, sub, sub departments, overlapping departments?

Multitudes.

A creepy alphabet soup.

EPA, FCC, FDA, FBI, NSA, DOJ, DOE, HUD, OSE, DOL, IRS, COB, VA, DOT, and quite a few others like DHS. This is the Department of Homeland Security, over Customs and Boarders, ICE, TSA, as well as, more than I can list or comprehend. An enormous department.

DHS is younger than most of my children.

All these acronym groups jockey for position and all hold out their hands as beggars for more, much more RESOURCES. That means money for salaries, health and retirement benefits, cool computers, vehicles, weapons and all kinds of other stuff.

Seems as if each State decided to create their own departments for enforcement. Good to have a backup. But many of those States need a bailout as they made commitments decades ago to pay retired employees the majority of their pay check until they die, plus their very high health insurance premiums (HEALTHCARE) for life. Only problem, the states did not fund the dollars for these expenses. Billions and billions. They are not an island to themselves. The federal government has unfunded entitlements to the tune of trillions.

What song would fit the choreography for scourge?

Got to love the government. Seems the only answer is currency reevaluation.

GOOD GOLLY MISS MOLLY.

A shifting world and unchartered territory.

Why not just get rid of this representative constitutional form of government, with real rights for the individual, and open the spigot wide for the sinister greedy, never satisfied, law makers and enforcers, to do as they will. Make this Republic into a true-blue Democracy. The majority will rule by the whims of unconfirmed social media posts and by the super-duper NETWORKS, these are those who bow down and sell themselves to the ratings of the advertiser driven system.

The product pushers, THOSE WHO SELL THEIR SHIT, through video, print or online, pay the bills for all the free information peddled. Seems fine if news came in a straight honest and unbiased fashion, but no, personal slanted editorial, seems to have taken over in spades.

GOTCHA, used to be the by-line of investigative reporting, now it is personal, genuine with real destruction. An undeniable and grievous fact and don't get me started on the great military industrial complex or the professional political class who are beholden not to constituents, but to their own hubris.

Here is a thought in this unchartered territory, let's get rid of names. Sticks and stones may break my bones but names will never hurt me, went out the back-door years ago, maybe decades. Proof, the children's rhyme is false.

Why don't we all gather together like a sweet cuddly community of individual isolated souls, from all kinds of backgrounds, nationalities, social economic differences, likes, hopes, fears, talents and dreams, pull together, lick our fingers in collective unison to see which way the political wind blows and create massive new sweeping laws on our own. Get rid of the representatives, I think only ten percent approve of them anyhow.

One raging problem would be "THE MANAGERS," those who in the end execute and enforce our untainted democracy. Another blaring issue would be minority rights, individual rights, protections for the forty-nine percent who voice, think, believe different from the massive majority held by the fifty-one percenters.

Abolish the electoral college, make the supreme court fifty or sixty judges. Why should Delaware, Montana, Wyoming and Rhode Island have two senators? California has fifty-four congressional representatives, Wyoming only one, but they each have two senators. Why and how? Make this whole vast, sea to shining sea, with purple mountains majesty, one big fat pure democracy.

No need to register to vote, no need for polling stations.

Oh wait, as an actual democracy, instead of a constitutional representative republic, the masses would make all the decisions and take none of the responsibility. That being said, the fifty-one percent could vote to get rid of the Judicial branch along with the legislative. Why stop there. Abolish the bill of rights. You know the amendments to the constitution, stating clearly, WHAT the GOVERNMENT CAN NOT DO. The amendments chaining the hands of those with power. Think about it, politicians would become extinct. No need for them in a straight democracy.

A pleasant thought.

Universal state-run healthcare for every beating heart. One payor, one system for hundreds of millions. My only recommendation is look at "Medicare" as the system for "ALL," and decide if that archaic under-funded, over regulated, nineteen sixties program is the one for all. Part A, Part B, Part D, are odd components.

Is healthcare a right? Life, Liberty and the Pursuit of Happiness seemed declared rights.

Why only healthcare? Maybe all banks, insurance companies, tele communication, (CELL PHONE's), airlines, food production, energy, the great military industrial complex, film studios, social media companies, housing, grocery stores, are another place for a one government run system.

A real ONE payer system.

One government film studio, social media company, airline, bank, cell phone provider, landlord and healthcare system, all free. The right to food, water, transportation, housing seem to be more of a right than HEALTHCARE, after all not everyone is sick all the time. All need water, food and shelter. These seem to be actual necessaries, you know RIGHTS.

A never-ending list.

In a straight democracy, the fifty percent, plus one will decide and the millions of the forty-nine percent have to go along. No more need for sixty percent or two thirds.

It might be the Antifascists, who for some odd reason, prove themselves to be the worst type of ugly Fascists, could pull together a simple majority and take over. Or the religious hypocrites who fight against abortion and fight equally diligently for the State to carry out government sanctioned executions. On the other hand, maybe a coalition could form out of diverse groups, Anti Socialist and Socialists, Anarchists and Pacifists, Conservatives and Liberals. Progressives and Libertarians. Millennials and the Baby Boomers. Mammoth corporations and Enormous government. Oh, wait, we already have that one.

Either way the Dye is cast, the answer is blowing by a fiery infused twisted wind. Change is under way.

We do have very clear experience with government run healthcare. They have been doing it for decades. The poor have coverage under Medicaid, the old under Medicare and the veterans under the VA. Now the one step above the poor have The Affordable Care Act, (OBAMA CARE). Only problem, the massive swiping law made a few universal specifics to all HEALTH INSURANCEC PLANS, Healthcare not insurance, forget about it. The government subsidize premiums, Big Insurance has their hands tied, but will not go under with the backing of Big Government as long as all plans include the ESSENTIAL BENEFITS. You know the ones in the thousands of pages in the bill signed into law. ESSIENTIAL, for every health insurance plan across the country without question and they subsidized the higher than poor and lower than the rich. It means these people under two hundred and fifty percent of the poverty level get free cash paid on their behalf to BIG INSURANCE. The above poor but below rich pay little while the government sends millions of dollars to insurance companies. Back in 2010 the talking points said, lower premiums, more access and everyone can get covered. A decade later premiums for a high-deductible plan costs more than a thirty-year mortgage.

What a great law.

Oh, and more people are uninsured.

Brilliant.

Medicaid had a fix which happened thirty years ago. The statement made went like this, "We saved Medicare." A simple fix, pay doctors less, only problem when it came to paying less, the politicians looked bad, they lust for reelection don't ya know, so for three decades when the budget comes for a vote, the fix is in and the can is kicked down the road for another day.

That being said the budget of the Federal Government does no take place, not for years and years. No budget only what they call it a "Continuing Resolution."

Keep over spending by trillions.

Yippie.

These are the people who need more power.

Oh, and one of the benefits of Medicare is the state funded care facilities. Medicare pays only certain amounts for certain lengths.

MEDICARE for all, yee-haw and giddy up.

The program is massively under-funded and archaic. It will be great if everyone has it. The majority want it, if they only knew what it is.

THE OLD FOLK HOMES we all heard about. They exist in every community across this great Land of the Free and Home of the Brave. From coast to coast, in every valley, nock and cranny on this awesome continent.

Everywhere.

They call them homes, not prisons, homes. They cannot go free, stuck separated from loved one's being looked after by untrained minimum wage workers to CARE for them. Government funded. Did I mention how the STATE, THE STATE, THE STATE, sent thousands of sick and weak, infected, by the PANDAMIC virus, back into lonely rooms, cared for by the ill-equipped and under paid workers while those infected spread the virus and they died with an inability to catch a last struggling clear breath?

Think about it. No breath. Suffocating, because you are old and under the authority of the STATE, while the governor stroked his Viagra infused third leg under the table, giving a daily briefing, "UPDATE" about lowering the curve with one true blue selfish interest. The hope to go to the top of the list for the possible next runner up for PRESIDENT OF THE UNITED STATES, four years from now, the next term. What a crock of shit and shame on him and all the deceptive types sticking their brown noses up his ass.

All of those self-focused, proud, small minded prostitutes.

Many thousand died, how do I know it is true? They said so. Those poor elderly human beings, from what they called the GREATEST GENERATION, suffered and died without their loved ones nearby, able to place a hand or brow on their head or arm as death and the grave walked in to have the final victory and they passed to another realm.

Trust the government and give them complete authority, YIPPE, plus an upbeat YAHOO you may die with a false sense of how GOVERNMENT is the answer, but trust me you will be massively lacking and wishing as you cannot suck in a clean breath of life-giving air. Die, forgotten and become a statistic.

One of thousands and thousands. All the poor souls who grieve with unconscionable pain do not forget.

How about if I get a bit provocative?

Taking a side note and going down a path.

I twist and spin in defeat although death and the grave do not have the final word. Victory is on the other side.

The governors and the orange president, the executives, are guilty but uncountable. Shame on them and their sick political points. This new world has shifted on the axis, tilting to terrifying, surreal, one ups, poll driven talking points. TALKING POINTS?

This is the new reality. Law-makers are subservient. Why do they still get paid and have bloated staffs? An unanswered question lingering in the ethos. But trust me, they will not pack up and go home. No way they will see the Writing on the Wall calling them to beg for forgiveness, bow down and accept their extinction. No, and by no means the political prostitutes will not only put the next three generations in debt as they smile and look for stokes on their pointy hollow haughty heads. They cannot help themselves; they have to over spend today more than ever. No matter it will leave a crushing burden on the shoulders of countless grandchildren's, grandchildren, of unimaginable debt. The here and now is all that matters, plus the repayment for their frivolous, gorging, off the charts spending will come due after these spenders are long gone and it has been happening for generations. Legislative, public servants, remember hold the purse strings for the good of the public. This is why they have been spending all the billions in excess funds taken in for the last half century from Social Security and Medicare. You know all the dollars needed to pay the commitments made to pay the for the entitlements? They spent it all and more, so much more, trillions and trillions more. A trillion here and a trillion there, and you may be talking real money. How much did this country owe in the seventies, the eighties and now under the orange man? Doesn't matter back then, it is twenty-eight trillion now and the commitments the hoard of silver tongued, LAW MAKERs, made for the last fifty years so they would feel good about their selfless service to the public while they ate like fat cats and smiled for the cameras.

Mindboggling.

Don't worry, the generations yet to come will be more than happy to work their fingers to the bone and tails off so enough taxes are auto drafted from their labor and from the sweat of their brow. These not yet conceived or born new tax payers will gladly pay it all back no questions asked. They will speak with reverence of all the SPEAKERs of the house and the majority LEADERs of the Senate, from all the parties, oh, excuse me, the two hypocritical parties. Oh, and wait, all the PRESIDENTs who made their executive branch grow and grow and grow with power, authority, with massive investigators, lawyers with subpoena powers back by the credit and full power of the government of the United States of America. The next generation will gather around the campfire, hold hands and sing Kumbaya.

Baby boomers, Gen X, Gen Y, divided by two. Gen Y.1 and Gen Y. 2 and Gen Z.

Forget the boomers they are old, self-focused and arrogant proud and entitled. So, it comes down to those born back in the Seventies, eighties, nineties, and after the millennium.

Interesting, the makers of law, give themselves defined benefit pension plans and super sweet private HEALTHCARE, that is health INSURANCE, with massive premiums paid by, you guessed, borrowed money. Some would say taxes, but no, they spent those taxes on all the government programs. Debt is for the extras these keepers of the governmental purse strings, have to have. No MEDICARE for the LAW MAKERS, EXECUTIVES and JUDGES.

Why has this government over spent one thousand billion dollars (One Trillion) a year for the last fifteen years? They took in between two and three trillion a year during this decade and a half, but always spent one trillion more. Why? Well, it seems clear. The entitlements, these are the commitments, the guarantee, the sure pure bet, millions were force to make, those mandatory deductions from their paychecks. Both, the employer and the employees, by gun point, paid taxes for Social Security and Medicare. For eighty years for Social Security and fifty years for Medicare. The rubber will hit the road sending terrifying deadly deep skid marks across the entire economy because the spenders could not help to restrain themselves. Don't worry they will blame others they always do. Interest rates will rise and the piper will come calling in a painful way. But hey, the call has been going out for decades.

The unfunded entitlement programs are the issue.

Unfunded to the tune of TRILLIONS.

But we need every one of the FOUR MILLION federal employees. We have to spend a trillion dollars more than we take in, because today is more important than tomorrow.

What the HELL?

Who are these people sucking off the nipple of the tax payors? Shame on them.

There is a ramble.

Only an illustration of so many more.

RAMBLE two.

A whacked-out diatribe. An embarrassing rant.

To make a sharp heinous pointed accusation fit into a round cube, I balance between way back when I needed to put a dime in a phone booth on the side of the road to make a call, instead of flowing my thumb over a glass face device to see, hear, listen and learn from the greatest education source ever available to a generation.

It is easy to believe life and existence is some esoteric painful comic joke, but let's gets real, facts are facts, how we decide makes a difference. Wishing and hoping for certain outcomes are only a dry embryonic spit into the eye of an intense overwhelming hurricane of the unbelievable. More than useless. Such is the way of all our collective existence we each share without question or ability to influence. What a great life, and at the same time painful, bound together in some mystical illusion human beings need to contemplate, bend their will to and accept.

Prosperity may be the shiny golden ring from the carousel because our luckless opportunity allowed us to not pluck one of hundreds for a brass ring? Does blessing come from luck or another source? Born rich and privileged? Born in squalor, back against the granite scared wall of hopeless despair? Is there a difference? Sure, but the external world is blind unable to turn inward, focused on the minor, small worthless emotional issues unable to see with true clarity. So many blind guides stumble and take multitudes into the depths of outer darkness leading to a bottomless pit because of their false seductive luring twisted fingers. A thumbs up or a click to get more views? What a fantastic world. Can any of us not be proud or boastful? On the other side of the coin could be opportunity. Humiliation, being mocked, looked down on, belittled comes with significant difficulties. It hurts. Our bodies do not feel the pain, we do. Pride will not bring gratitude. Compassion cannot arrive on the clipped wings of arrogance.

We all have choices, many are easy, most are hard, but when we do not look, or buck against the cards dealt in the hand of our existence worry about the aces coming face up for others, a sweet spot unfolds with the winning cards for no other reason than unexplainable chance, seasoned with a higher purpose we need to discover throughout our journey in this lonely life.

I, in this world, with all the ridiculous whacked out philosophies propagated by small, pitiful, highly educated, and other pointy headed talkers and anxiety driven self-promoting square heads, drive me to a place I could go bonkers.

The choices we make, do not overlook nor do they make clear the motive behind decisions. So powerful and life changing. A yes or no can contain more influence than the second it takes, could ever convey. A real problem in life.

Just a question I pounder and scream internally with inaudible fiery to the ends of the earth against an eternal blank utterly soundless room where ears do not hear, where backs turned centuries before I came into existence.

One consolation we all share is the common reality we live in the same time in a universal, collective sinking boat, twisting, turning and pounding against the power of our life we have no control over.

Many have really cool degrees from dead leaf institutions which is the sickest form of prostitution. They should all pull their skirts up and entice the government to take a ride, get their rocks off, feel good and fund the hypocritical whores, who bellow out about the plight of migrants, all the while they hide behind false blindness sitting on billions in reserve as the poor massive die in sinking inflated rafts hoping for a new and better life.

Higher education is one thing, producing unfulfilled covetousness in the heart of countless human beings is worse. See, but don't touch, until you pay. Want, want, want. Playing on desire. The product pushers are everywhere. They even use their slimy ways to target small children in grotesque ways all for money. Money is the deal. Got to have it and you need more, much more, so you can have what teased your eyes to covet.

The advertisers who pay for the eye balls, lust for those who watch, listen, to get stirred up in the childish fake battles falling so short of the painful, actual point. Academics do not feed the real poor, nor do their small-minded hopeless philosophies lift the needy from squawker. Can corporations keep making their stock holders profits as the GREAT MILITARY COMPLEX sucks their thumbs while spilling their unfertilized load over the dying and dead eggs across the earth? It is proven, they are inept, flabby, false wizards behind a flimsy curtain, small and afraid with secret powerless protection lifting their limp middle finger high and wide. Can I get a thumbs up or more FOLLOWERS? Only a cynical, poignant question.

Disgusting!

Hypocrites!

Bastards!

A pox on both their houses. But I digress, my bad.

Makes me want to run through the streets with sack cloth and ashes screaming, I-CHABOD!

What in the world? WHAT'S GOING ON???

I am small, only one troubled soul. Too small to know, but great enough to call out all the slimy pieces of shit on both sides of the aisle who bend and break to special interests. SPECIAL. Who are the interests? Complete pieces of shit. Agenda driven, singularly focused, profit driven, one sided, might have some well-meaning ideas but are duped and deceptive, hyper convulsive college graduates who bought into worthless dead philosophies on one side or the other.

Fight for choice. Fight for life. Stand against abortion or open it wider. Defend government sanctioned murder, or picket against the death penalty? Issues, big issues, so worthless because our founders wrought words on paper. Seems good and honorable, I get it but let's be clear, times changed and camps rose up and became battle grounds. The reason the courts have risen high. The rule makers live afraid behind high walls and do not get together and work things out for the mass of human beings all around.

WOWEE. SHUCKS. A great new world and I am only a minuscule voice, but I have a keyboard, so I will press on. My rambling mind and traveling bone has power to get the best of me, but I will work to get back on track of my actual ramble.

I have stood for decades against the lie. It tries, with a sneaky manipulation, to push down, screw in with a deceptive effort to take up residence in me. It has not been easy, but I worked to stand firm, the best I can, against the tricks and power.

With the changes in the world I suffered under sophisticated and sinister shifts, pivots, to take me down into an unhealthy pit of despair. I can say it has not been an easy battle. Many times, I came out on the shorter end of the stick, slammed under the onslaught, behind the eight ball. Creamed and disillusioned, back on my heels stumbling for one breath, but time makes a way.

I am here still.

Similar to the way I fought to keep horrible headaches from taking over my life, I did not let the lie overtake me. Not completely. Nothing to be proud of, I understand. I only state with apprehension I could find myself turned inside out. A war I will stay engaged in until a time I cannot comprehend.

The opposite of this is the true and clear weakness many and most human beings chose. Bitterness, unforgiveness, hatred and blame. The almost universal declaration. "IF ONLY THEY WOULD HAVE DONE THIS OR THAT THAN I WOULD BE HAPPY. We are unable to find contentment in blaming others.

I learned early on bitterness, does nothing for those you blame, it only affects you in a clear negative fashion. The one clear memory, besides so many deeper ones is, "If you point a finger at someone else three fingers point back at you". Simple, I agree, cheesy maybe, but profound and anchored in truth.

I stated these words verbally with genuine ignorant sincerity, "I have the answer for your problems."

Shame on me.

Without opinion and a degree of shaky humility, desiring to show value to everyone I encounter, I turned the page of my life and utterly failed.

Then I lost grip on reality.

I came back to a place of semi normality on a quasi-lucid balancing beam with a brilliant and naïve thought. "The processionals can diagnosis me and set out a treatment plan." How wrong and ignorant. The simplicity, I understand it should be the perfect place to get on the right track for a solution, but we live in the north western hemisphere where the desire for profits have a powerful incentive.

"The need to be happy, successful, healthy, prosperous," is a western society lie, indoctrinated over a few hundred years to think we are the best, others are less, living in a literal blink in history on a floating planet at the bottom side or an infinite universe which does not end.

There you have it.

I am very saddened to sit back and see how this type of rambling, wondering, weird diatribe came out. I am learning to overcome, calm down and avoid many of these. I used them as an example in the hopes it many open a wider corridor where I can see, recognize and overcome the onslaught by letting the crazy walk by without engagement.

I am doing better with the rambling thoughts, but I also have to deal with the issues which come from nowhere at any time. Here is one as an illustration.

An ISSUE FOCUSED EVENT.

I went to the beach with the seventh of the seven, the best of all of us. The rest of the seven would agree wholeheartedly. There is no question, and no shame. The consensus is undeniable with scientific data driven truth.

Thank God for His Mercies.

Anyhow, I found myself in another state, still twisting and turning, fully engaged as the seventh drove us to the beach to visit and connect with some cousins.

I remained in the hotel room, giving a wide berth for my beautiful daughter to enjoy and vacation. As the sun rose high in the sky, I stepped out on the patio at the beach and witnessed a scene I want to forget. Without judgement I will replay the specifics.

A thin man with a broken leg in a full cast sat back while a heavy-set woman spit and smoked, sipping out of a paper bag, wondering around unaware of anything outside her peripheral self-focused vision. A twenty something mother sat with them while her daughter toddled and stumbled about near a baby boy who crawled around on the sand. The mother got up and went to her hotel room. I stood one floor up, on a balcony, and did not hear if she told the other adults to watch the kids, if she did it do not work. The toddler started to wail and set off across the bumpy sand falling and biting the dust on the grit of the sand, but she pressed on with one goal, get to MAMA. The baby crawled after his sister and stopped each time the tiny girl fell. The wet tears mixed with sand turned the young child's face into a filthy mess. She made it to a cement walking path and found her footing and went out of sight. The baby continued to crawl after his sister and onto the sand spilled cement. A painful sight. The two adults sat and talked without the slightest interest as if these two struggling children did not exist. The mother came back with the girl in her arms, scooped up the boy and went back to the blind adults.

It is hard to describe the vast and unbalanced emotions spiking and shooting through me. This situation is not so horrible or out of the norm in so many places. Kids are resilient and they bounce back, nothing bad really took place, but I spun like a broken kite in the wind without a string. A powerful blowing wind which could have uprooted me, throwing me reeling and flapping in an endless hurricane. I know, sometime removed and looking back, my internal struggle came with preconceived judgements, the adults not seeing, not hearing and not caring and the painful struggle of the two tiny little humans balanced against the mother who came back with open arms and no frustration or worry, just another day at the beach, but I became filled with more than two stories, or outlooks and almost came unglued.

Tearing the building down, screaming at the top of my lungs or wail with grief were the first three emotions which pelted me, the other thirty-three are not worth being addressed. I did not go berserk, nor did I fly off the deep end.

I have no balancing scale against two little, struggling human souls on a faraway BEACH who happened to be in my sight for less than a few minutes against the vast, wide open cravenness divide with DISCONNECTING COMMON threads across the whole globe turning together in a clear unknowing sympathy no one can hear.

Interesting enough for me, a simple minded, confused minded INDIVIDUAL, there are deeper issues which need attention.

My issues, are not not societies issue they are mine and mine alone. I need to deal with the problems, recognize and not blow my stack in public, in the real world. Hold firm, hold back and stand on guard. Settle down and chill, get a grip and relax, until waives of irritation and instability slowly subside giving way to a possibility of normality.

A quandary.

So much harder than it looks.

One of the most painful parts of my mental health recovery or understanding, recognition, is how uncontrolled the rambling thoughts, twisted ideas, absurd issues, all come against me without warning and so damn fast. Lighting speed, digging deep with real emotional ups and downs causing horrible physical reactions throughout my whole being, and they linger longer than they should.

Longer than should be.

Much longer.

Thoughts which cause feelings.

Here is a turn of subject, going down another lane.

I can make myself think, imagine, ponder and fantasize on numerous graphic thoughts which in turn can make my heart putter and my groins swell with temporary ecstasy. It is easy to shift and tilt my thoughts and create vivid images, in an imaginary make-believe realm where I make up, on the fly, an elaborate world with specific components of music, storybook dialog, set in a pristine scene of touching and stroking with a wild mixture, of beautiful and soft, sweet temptresses with power to fulfill every one of my sexual dreams. Fantasies, MY MIND CREATES very elaborate situations tilted in my favor for my satisfaction.

With eyes closed, fully engaged in imagination, in the darkness, the secret place where profound multi colored motion pictures spin and turn, in slow soft motion bringing a rising place of arousal to a point of gratifying sensations with quivering, pulsating, buzzing stimulation through every nerve ending and ricocheting through the recesses of every pour ending, makes me ask two questions.

Is this crazy? Is this mental illness?

Some have called me crazy, but they would have to admit they do this same thing, some more than others, but I am not alone in this well practiced temporary gratifying release through imagination.

Thoughts produce feelings and physical release.

Unspoken in polite society, but commonly understood. The vast majority, across the globe for centuries, I would conclude without taking a poll, do and did this same thing.

NO SHAME, only a factual observation.

The end result is temporal. It feels great, really great, but it does not last and it does not bring actual fulfillment.

After I eat a meal, I feel full then I find myself hungry again.

When I am thirsty, I drink and I feel satisfied and filled up, until the thirst returns.

I long for stuff and when I make a purchase a buzz or slight lingering piece of joy ensues. Then I look again for other products to BUY.

On the other side of the equation, my mind can settle on disturbing thoughts, not fantasy, but just as potent and destructive. Replaying conversations with others, hoping for an alternative outcome. Worrying about the future when it has not happened and may not. Thoughts which cause grief, sadness, anger, a desire for revenge, get even or win, all seem to be part of the human experience. These cause unpleasant, non-gratifying feelings, but they do not seem to out of the norm.

A painful truth for sure, but not crazy.

On the other hand, I have come to discover I contained a few outside the norm issues which appear to be abnormal and problematic.

Not a common shared experience.

Voices, Shadows, Faces, Phobias.

Unhealthy thoughts which for me turn down a darker path than our shared experience, of visual fantasy or tendencies toward the negative, are more dangerous and severe. Explicit ACCUSATIONS, alluring tricks, downright deceptions come from nowhere and pound me with dark intent. I also hear, at times, what I call Circus Talk. Incoherent statements with no reasonable interpretation. Weird and very unsettling. But the worst, are the voices, in my head, stating plain sharp allegations against all I hold dear. My deep-seated beliefs, my understanding of reality using thorny persuasive attacks. These remained under the radar and unheard or unrecognized while I existed high in wild manic living, only popping an ugly head of a lying tongue above the horizon, at diverse times. My hyper busy mind racing a million miles an hour in daily ritual of risk taking and vision casting, allowed the unseemly aggressive voices to remain unacknowledged and elsewhere.

Unheard and unrecognized.

Since coming to an all stop with unlimited time to pounder and contemplate, a sinister unleashing unfolded with purpose driven, unbenevolent, clipped accusatory words speaking with clear and unmistakable determination, although on the outskirts of recognition. One liner's, direct and poignant statements, with a singular purpose. To rattle and unsettle my stability, resolve, sanity.

The lie lingered high with power, but on the dark fringes waiting to strike. These unambiguous threating mental attacks came, and still come at any time, out of an empty space. When I answer, I find myself in a losing battle grasping and scrapping, so I am learning to let them pass by without engagement.

It would be less difficult to overcome if these voices were not so personal. The effectiveness and influence would contain less sharpened teeth. But I confess, I am stymied at times, wishing to give in and struggle to stand firm. Some days nothing, others an onslaught which causes me to stumble, but I get up slightly stronger each time, more stable with a stouter balance in my step and at times weaker and ready to cave in as I hold to a singular truth.

A voice in my head will not kill me.

It should be a simple task to turn a blind eye and not listen. Most times I can, others, not so easy. The only power these voices hold is what I allow and give into.

How I respond.

A battle in the mind causes physical, emotional and spiritual difficulties. Fatigue, fear, doubt. Taking thoughts captive and setting my mind on things above have proven to produce value, but it is difficult to guard against every flaming thought, especially when they shift and turn, evolve and come from different directions without warning and new artillery.

These arguing voices are internal which is outside the norm. You tell people you are hearing voices and watch out. I do not hear conversations or multiple mocking and tormenting chatter, only specific targeted, aggressive pointed one-line sentences.

"See this proves your wrong."

"Your children will suffer."

And the big one:

"This proves God does not exist. Give up."

These accusatory internal attacks have been with me since way back when and have remained under the wire as if defeated in a dormant place for large seasons of my life only to raise their ungodly heads at a moment's notice. I hear them only in my head with ability to bring destruction and chaos with the end result of mockery, being outcast from society and the unpleasant possibility of involuntary lockdown. So, I tread lightly with open ears and a resilient heart in the reality of my own personal battle.

We do not war against flesh and blood, but against principalities of the air.

Shadows.

I do not see people who are not there, nor do I talk out loud to non-existent beings no one else can see. I do, on the other hand, have an issue with shadows. Thin dark lines standing outside my periphery. It would be easy to bypass these immaterial, unreal anomality's as what they are, Illusions. Quick, vapors of nothingness without quantifiable mass and I do, for the most part after facing the influx of experience. After I physically jerk and then recognize the shadow is an illusion which caused an actual jolt in my body.

In quicker than a second, I see, feel and contemplate the first scene of a horrific movie all in bright definition and clarity. This is hard to explain. At times as I drive through a four-way section in any given town with a green light for my passage, I sense first, then I see outside my vision, a faded shadow in the form of a dark streak in a blink. A physical jerk takes place in my body, like an electrical probe touched my side and I feel the arch. No pinch or heat, only the jolt. Then I see the story. Quick and fast. A split second, but detailed and ominous.

Three examples.

A shriveled white-haired woman, both hands on the wheel, in a dark green late model Buick running the red-light and plows into the side of my car. She is sad about her husband who died recently and over her children who rarely visit. The crumpled metal, smell of smoking rubber and shock all bent together.

Bingo.

A young mother dressed in a purple and yellow sweat suit rolling a three wheeled buggy, with her new-born child across my path. BAM, I crash through with full horrifying carnage, feeling the pain of destruction and the sorrow wanting to go back and crash into a pole instead.

Two teenagers riding skateboards, collide into each other and the weaker one falls in front of my moving vehicle. Crunch, a scream and screeching tires loud and horrifying all in less than a second.

Very unsettling.

Shadows of only a faded line just behind my sight with very clear and detailed components which are not real, do not exist, but dig deep in my body and memory.

I see, hear, feel and live in the aftermath which does not go away as fast as they arrived. False reality with lingering physical and emotional sensation as I continue down the road. I have only told two people about this anomaly or delusion which makes me never want to get behind the wheel again as long as I live. I drive slower now, cognizant, on guard, friendly, open to let others in, thankful to have such a wonderful opportunity to come and go and see the world. I have regrets I spent so many years zipping in and out, angry, not enjoying the gift of transport. I now smile if someone flips me off and I wish them, in my heart, peace and rest with the possibility of a place of contentment.

My faith knows no bounds.

A better way to drive and live at least from my point of view.

Slow and sweet.

These shadows or dark lines hit me outside a moving vehicle as well. In a grocery store, gas station, bank, the post office. The same jolts spark's in me with a detailed discernment of the life story of someone who does not exist. I think this is why I took my glasses off back when so I could not see the expressions of real people and to make the shadows go blank.

Only a discernment I am unable to quantify.

Faces.

In the dark of night, with my eyes closed in preparation for a time of hibernation, called sleep, I experience at times, unblinking eyes staring directly at me. Full faces with intricate detail looking directly into me. No words, no conversation, only a perfectly focused face I have not seen before. People I do not know, looking at me. This is more than odd I understand, call it weird, creepy, but just the same I cannot deny it. Faces, many faces in full definition with all the lines of emotions, telling stories and asking for help or acknowledgement in their gaze. I hear no words, but sense and feel the message, the life story and most are less than hopeful. The emotions run the gambit from euphoria to bitter sorrow. Smiles are far less than fear or torment, so much fear and terror. Anxiety seems to be the least powerful. Grief and sorrow the greatest. Many times, I opened my eyes in the dark, rub my head and shack out the cobwebs and it does the trick. No more faces, no more feelings, no trouble. Other times I go deep and wait and watch, feel and sense as dozens of faces of complete strangers flick on by, telling their stories with only a facial expression and their eyes. The unblinking eyes tell the story so deeply, a freshly polished novel is available for print and distribution. Where, when, how, without the who. I do not need to know who; the eyes tell more.

The best way I can describe this is a deck of cards all with a vast variety of face cards of real people from all over the world.

Old and young, more than Black or White, Asian or Hispanic features. An endless supply, of races, sizes, shapes, geographic location and feelings. So many feelings, such deep feelings. A bottomless ocean could not contain all the feelings.

I took a night to watch and wait as the faces passed by as long as I could without opening my eyes and shaking it off. I am unable to give the number of faces or the length of time. Numerous for an extended period. I watched and felt all the emotions, interested in why and what. The experiment did not turn out well. I went deeper and started to believe I could travel the globe in my mind using an internal sophisticated global positioning system and travel to the exact location on the planet, enter the home of those before my view and communicate. Bangladesh, India, the Gaza strip, New York, Montreal, Scotland, Brazil, Western Africa, Yemen, all over.

I practiced and traveled in my mind to sail, without an anchor, or guide post, across the vast planet, to a specific room in the Barrios of Rio de Janeiro, a church Sierra Leone, a penthouse in the upper west side of NYC, a hospital in Calcutta to find the face looking at me. Flying around the globe in my mind.

Zing.

No need to pinch out or zoom in.

I never had any conversation and I tend to not take a ride of this nature very often. Mostly I pray and allow my heart to open up with compassion. I have no clue of the meaning or purpose, I can only state, this happens more nights than not. Actually, whenever I close my eyes for a period of time. I also realize this anomality or delusion, psychosis, is abnormal, so I mostly keep it hidden and try not to indulge.

Seeing faces, you do not know, but believe you can reach out to, boarders very close to the edge of crazy, maybe a few steps over.

Watch out.

Phobias.

Most of my life I not only lived in a manic state, but I played as well. Fast and high. I rode high flying roller-coasters, jumped from bridges into rushing waters, climbed trees to the top, flew down thin dirt paths on a bicycle with a death-defying cliff on one side and a mountain on the other. Without fear I took physical risks to the max and never considered the consequences.

No Fear.

Those days have gone by and I find myself living now with an unhealthy and unreasonable, although very real, terror of heights. Being afraid of high places seems understandable and not outside the norm. The issue in me goes way further, far beyond, all the way to the edge, of an utter irrational and illogical place. I can state this with a clear sober minded recognition, but it does not change the physical horrible feelings or terror when I know, logically, I should not.

Walking across a dam, with water on one side, a massive precipice on the other, and thirty feet from either side, a physical panic rises through my blood stream. Hiking near a cliff is nearly unbearable. I drove from Southern California along the coast and I wanted to scream, pull over and cry out for help. The coastal highway could be the most majestic sights in the world. I almost lost my mind. With guard rails on both sides and four lanes, I squeezed my left eye shut so I could not see the post card perfect view even though I remained three lanes away from guard rails. I could not look.

Irrational and illogical.

I am still working to get a grid of this abnormality I need to overcome or I may find myself house bound.

Early Exposure and Fleshly indulgence.

I need to bring up and expose an issue I have shared with a few others over the years with little or no value. I lived in south Minneapolis in a middle-class neighborhood of unique homes built after world war one. The baby boom happened after world war two and over a decade and a half of prosperity went into high gear with bright shining new kinds of promising opportunity and exploded all around and there were kids, so many little human beings birthed and running around everywhere. THE BABY BOOM. I am the last of this mysterious group. Born the last year of the BOOM.

As a young wiper snapper, five years of age, I cut my teeth, scuffed my knees, climbed trees and PLAYED all around the neighborhood. No one worried, no one asked questions, and the adults held an open trust for some odd reason. A wide-open trust. Nothing bad will happen.

After breakfast the doors flew open and all the kids intermingled wide and far, until the lunch or dinner bell rang to come home. More kids than you could count all hit the streets and interacted on a daily basis. No adults and no rules. The variety of adolescent's and mid teen kids flooded the streets in a two-block radius and had fun. Lots of fun and there was plenty in every direction. Twelve in one family, eight kids in another, six in ours and so on. A catholic neighborhood where more seemed to be better. More seemed worthy for conceit. The poor mothers who birthed the broods, God forgive, and worse, how sad, for those who could not conceive. GOD have Mercy.

Times have changed.

The houses all built with full basements also sat between the street and a thin broken alley behind each for access to the one-car garage and trash removal. The alley is where we all seemed to PLAY, and play we did. I can still smell and see the abandoned school bus in the alley on the other block from my home. I am not sure how, but I found myself inside with a dozen or so other kids. I knew right away I was the youngest by far, only five years old. The older kids lit and smoked and pulled out a bottle. Someone spun the thing and an assortment of demands took place. I have no recollection of specifics of the GAME, but I do recall being taken by one of the older girls into the crammed bathroom to carry out the dare. My recollection remains faded, but I still contain the powerful emotions from that far away day. Touching and feeling, those were the words. She touched, and I felt and the laughter when we came out sent a curious echoing reverberation around the mildew scented old gutted bus, I will never forget. I am not sure what the others did. I hold a shadowy recollection some of my siblings being in the bus on that day, but I struggle to remember which one or any other specifics. I only know I will never forget the day the lights came on. Girls are awesome, sweet, soft and mysterious. It has never left me.

Across the cosmos this truth must reverberate. At least from one viewpoint.

I still remember her name and face, the house she lived in and her large family. Years later, after we moved to the west coast, we took an annual pilgrimage back to the Twin Cities, and I always wanted to reconnect, but it so happens I was only a punk kid. She did not even give me the slightest of acknowledgement. I do not blame her. How sad. Two small children persuaded through peer pressure to go behind locked doors and do as told. Very sad and in my case a damaging fact.

A year or two later a family member diddled my teeny weenie and exposed me to full on nakedness. I have often wondered why and found out years later. We all have our own crosses to bare. I held an unhealthy blame for an extended period which I have come to understand only caused me trouble. This revelation did not come easy or quickly, it took me years to understand. All children see through their own eyes and most act without thought, so forgiveness plows the way.

At the age of thirteen, a very difficult time in life, an older girl in the neighborhood, actually right across the street from my home, used me like a discarded toy and I still have difficulty coming to grips with the experience. I struggled between my open acceptance and the gratification I received against a backdrop of molestation. As a junior high kid with a mother who cracked up, unable to pass a test and a bit horny to begin with, I became a sitting duck for a sexually aggressive and persuasive older neighbor to do with me as she willed.

Putty in her hands.

It went unrecognized at the time, but has messed in a profound way all these years since. I long felt it was my fault, looking back with years of life I know it wasn't. The perpetrator in guilty, not the victim. I did not feel like a victim as every boy in my school dreamed of such things. The dream turned out to be a kaleidoscope of miss matched ugly emotions with confusion lingering from the sinister acts and the spooky fact.

It must have been some type of game or twisted need to control, I am unable to say for sure. I can say orgasm became the most important part plain and simple. Feel good and get off, anywhere and at any place. In the dirty bathroom at a pizza parlor, under the bushes in the yard, behind the fence even right out in the open sometimes. Afterward I found myself treated like a stranger who did not even exist. Overlooked and put down, mocked actually. On two occasions, in a house with several other older boys, playing poker, getting high, this happened not in the bathroom, but in the other room open for everyone to see. I can still see the glee or power in having others who desired her watch without being able to touch. Mean and evil, as I became only a toy used to hurt others.

We were never a couple, never went out or steady, only a toy and a twisted broken master. She used me as a vessel for some screwed up reason and to torment others. I had several of those who stood in the distance and observed tell how much they hated me and how they hated her. I struggled to not agree with them. Ugly, humiliating, wrong with sexual gratification, very sick and I willingly participated as a perfect obedient toy.

Whenever and wherever.

Thirteen is a child.

As a boy who freely participated, but lacked understanding and felt like a man years before coming of age, without training, hidden, confused, used, it took me years to see the truth.

I allowed myself to be taken advantage of and deceived.

Since then I have come to understand I closed down and shut off my emotions. I never gave my heart to another. I said I did, but now I see I lied. Many who I know well have told me, they never knew me. I never opened, never shared the real me. I did not talk about myself to anyone. A problem which I am working to overcome. I listened like a champ to others with true compassion, and gave my best thoughts of wisdom or worse out of my lame opinions, without ever really giving my true self.

This is another large painful regret.

Friends, family, the Beautiful Perfect Seven, lived in a one-sided relationship around me. It is not their fault. I closed off the real me to their open hearts. Hidden in plain sight. I did not act with malice or some sinister plan or predetermined intention. A knee jerk reaction learned over years and very difficult to undo. I am trying. I have turned the page only to find a bright blank sheet with no lines or grids.

A bank slate and a slippery slope.

I have found out on my journey through experience and experiment, spilling your guts is not the first step toward openness and understanding. I found it out the hard way. Cooky talk is not a good place to let loved ones and friends gather a glimpse at the real you.

Sad but true.

I tented to hide and smile, listen and nod, but not open my heart. Now I am, here, out in the real world. It does not come easy as I tilted to silence and secrets for the majority of my life. If I open up to far or to fast the crazy starts pouring out, so there is a balance I am working to perfect.

A tender balance.

So here I am.

Phobias, faces, shadows, voices and lies have become a five-pointed star with the ability to create a trigger to spin me off axis and I need to stand firm, be aware, not react, not give recognition of the abnormal tweaked origins where these threats emerge from.

Five is not so bad. Could be worse and I have seen worse, so I remain thankful and prepared with no pride or hubris. The battle waged against me is formidable and deadly. I have several weapons, both defensive and a list with sharp offensive points.

I will lay them out the best I can. Many are not shiny or worth calling home about, but they are potent and strong, at least in my case.

In the mind.

The bulk of the issues hammering me and wanting to crush me to the dirt and turn my life to mush, exist only in my mind. The oddity of this realization came with some inconceivable components. I cannot say why, but I somehow felt as if the issues I found myself pelted by were all around me, not inside. When your body feels tension, fear, anxiety, anger, confusion, there is an illusion it comes from outside forces. Loss of a job, tragedy, someone else hurts you or from many other unknown points of society, there seems to be a place to blame. The fact is worse. Those hardships, painful interactions are external, but the real difficulty emerges internally. A horrible reality, but one worth investigating with the intend to overcome.

Both from me and from some other ethereal place, faces and phobias, voices and shadows and lies come in all shapes and sizes. Some from recognizable places, other from who knows where. Not reacting is my first line of defense. Let them flow, let them flow, walk on by. Come as they will without engagement seems to have a powerful value. It is uncomfortable and difficult, but somewhat effective in the short run. Buzzing anxiety and worry come flooding in as a physical byproduct and real with only a power to make me feel. The feelings suck, don't get me wrong, but will not kill me and they get worse if I try to make them go away.

Much worse.

I am working to not respond, not answer or acknowledge and I am finding a degree of release.

"Goodbye yellow brick road where the dogs of society howl."

Saying good bye, Sayonara, Adios, Von Buoyage, Good Riddance, does not work as well as it should. I wish it did, my oh my, how I do, but let's get real. Those with manners would take the hint. Crazy has no manners and walks in untrainable disobedience. Crazy needs to have its knees cut out and stomped to death. Only problem, overlooking, not drawing attention and giving zero acknowledgement seems to be the first line of defense.

Offense weapons.

Prayer.

Turning to the creator and lover of my soul, not in a posture of begging for release, but in acknowledgement of the majesty, omnipotent power and truth, is my first go to. I cannot keep my own heart beating nor can I turn a switch in my mind and stop an onslaught of nutty things, but I can turn to God with an open heart. Acknowledgement, love and gratitude. I do beseech on behalf of the Perfect Seven as I am unable to help myself.

Telling others.

Not all, but some of the issued attacking me I choose to verbally bring to the light with the three I trust. I do not do this all the time, only when it gets insurmountable. Interesting enough this option does not arrive as often. Be thankful for small miracles.

You.

I write down my struggles, thoughts, weirdness, lessons I am learning to YOU. Who are You, you may ask? Well you are YOU and I am me. Good to meet YOU. Written talk therapy has become a strong offensive practice I use by spilling my guts through typed words which gives me insight and a powerful release. Very powerful.

Thank YOU!

Setting my mind elsewhere.

I can do nothing about the incoming flaming missiles into my head so I look away without acknowledgement nor a fight. Instead I set my mind elsewhere. God as I said, the seven or course, the beauty found in nature, the awesome wonder of the universe, a Hot Fudge Sundae, to name a few. There is an endless supply of good things to think about.

Avoiding.

Political information and religious doctrine are unhealthy for me to engage with. I dabble at times to test the waters, but for the most part I avoid these. I look forward to a day when this may not be an issue, but until then I stand guard and watch out.

Music.

Instead of information and dogma, I turn on music. Thank God for music and the awesome brilliant, creative musicians around the world from times gone and today for sharing their gifts. So beautiful. So amazing. The variety is vast and powerful, with mixes of tempos and individual creativity. Fast, slow, up-beat, or ominous, music is one of the greatest gifts to my life. In the darkest hour of my mental crack up I came across a lifesaving group of musicians called PLAYING for CHANGE. I am unable to describe the impact these amazing people have had in my step toward stability. Tears well in my eyes and gratitude bulges in my heart at the thought of them.

God Bless Playing for Change.

Appreciation.

I take time to appreciate the endless supply of the blessings of life. Sight, sound, ability to walk, food, water, The Perfect Seven, friends, God's creation, technology, stories, movies, rest, laughter, the list goes on and on, and on. I take time to reflect and focus on the goodness of life. The beauty, the underserved gifts and unfathomable wonder of so much to appreciate helps me to settle down and gives some assembly of peace.

No Control.

I acknowledge and recognize I hold a speck of power or control over so few places in this big bad world. I do have authority over my front yard, my automobile, my body and mind, but other than those, very few.

It took me a very long time and going down a treacherous horrible winding road, to come to this simple truth.

We have very little control, but with responsibility and authority in specific area.

The Beautiful Perfect Seven.

For some out of the universe reason, a damaged, deceitful, incapable, uneducated, kid, received a priceless gift. The Beautiful SEVEN. How in the world and why? Hand the keys of a Bentley to a two-year-old. Give a billion dollars to a ten-year-old. Give Seven perfect souls to a broken man. Much more than I can bare. Certainly, more than I deserved, but hey, you need to put the best foot forward.

Looking back, I would have changed many things, actually the majority. I would have made my focus laser directed to the only real place I held true responsibility as the highest calling. The government, world affairs, religious differences, my opinions hold not power for change or control. They do not matter. My thoughts have no effect and do nothing. A spit into a rolling hurricane. A penny flung at a tornado. I wasted my energy, time, will power, focus on areas I held less than a thimble's worth of water to control. Talk, talk, talk in worthless philosophical discussions and arguments, which did nothing. NOTHING and so much talk.

REGRET, regret, regret.

The revelation of my short falls toward the Seven is almost unbearable.

Shame on me.

Making money, dreaming up new things, investing for a profit or loss, vain imagination, worthless philosophies, useless conversations, listening to the problems, worries, wounds of near strangers, stole from my children a fully engage and present father.

The one they needed.

Without sounding like a complete looser I will highlight an odd part of my nature. I had this weird ability, and still do in the mist of my current crazy place, an ability to turn the manic or psychosis off to engage in the small, but huge things my young children cared about. It is a bit of an on or off switch or some incongruent part of my nature, so the Seven, I believe would say things like, "you were a great dad", or "we love you, you gave us a good life," things along those lines, but after they fell asleep I stayed up, or got up early and created the next best thing. Then I put my all into seeing it come into this world and make money or achieve "SUCCESS." Over and over I did this. A better widget. I saw the light, the glory, the truth. This idea is outstanding.

Shit.

No going back, but what a temptation to imagine. So much I would change.

I would forgo my wild and crazy tendencies to roll the dice, and spent so much mind effort and money on the abstract. I would have told politics to go to hell and I would have said I don't care about religious doctrine and philosophy, plus a long list of other shortcomings, and I would have poured all that energy and resource into the BEAUTIFUL PERFECT SEVEN.

Well I went down a rambling road there when my intent held a purpose to give the list of offensive weapons I hold in my quiver.

A good example of where I am and where my mind can take detours.

Getting back on tract.

No Opinion.

I have been working diligently to not give any opinions. I use the phrase, "I'm sorry I have no opinion." I bite my tongue and do my best to listen with as much understanding as I can and keep my thoughts in check for the benefits of others.

Walk with compassion.

Judgment has proven to be an unhealthy part of my makeup. Having a predetermined value of others in a quick blink with no basis is a disgusting shameful way to live. It would be great if I could say with enthusiasm, I never judged others as quick as Lickety Split, but in my wildest dreams I could never come up with a convincing argument to overcome the over whelming truth and painful truth. I acted and walked as a wretched man. I size up, judged, looked down over my proud nose to put me up above so many in so many places at any given time.

A wretched man. A judgmental proud slacker.

I fight against my deceived nature to come into balance with truth. I am the wounded one. The broken soul. When I walk with focused compassion judgement fades in the background, opening up a bright opportunity for change and hope through acceptance of all I encounter. Whether by sight or actual engagement, I still feel a weird need or desire to pull out money or pour out my tweaked opinions, but I am learning to hold firm while I wait and watch and check my heart. I still need time and help with a wide boulevard of grace to maneuver and find a straight line to walk in a place of full inclusion and acceptance.

Compassion for others and recognition of my short comings has proven to contain value and a potent offensive weapon.

Spiritual Song.

Although I polluted myself with religious philosophy and doctrine, I will openly state I sang hundreds of spiritual songs many times, outstanding songs to the creator of my soul for decades. The tempos change up or down, but so many opened my heart wide and far. Ancient hymns, modern chores and wonderful spiritual songs. One well-known hymn crossed over from sacred to secular is, "AMAZING GRACE." Many can sing the first verse by memory whether or not they believe it. A spiritual song written by a British slave ship captain who repented and in sorrow of his own undeniable guilt, scripted the most recognizable spiritual song. There are hundreds of others which I learned and sing, in my mind and verbally at times as a profound and effective attack against the crazy flinging arrows against my soul.

Prayer, singing spiritual songs, holding my opinions in check, avoiding encumbrances, giving compassion, listening to exceptional music and living with appreciation in my heart are perfect parts of life to bring me to a place of balance and stability against the twisted, abnormal, tricky, sinister, accuser wanting to tempt me to fall down the cliff of insanity.

I use the weapons as if my life depends on them.

With no doubt the battle needs forceful aggressive effective counter attacks.

An undeniable truth.

Don't worry about me, chose your own weapons to defeat these unseen disgusting threats which rage against all human isolated souls.

We all have a path to travail.

Balance. Stability. Longevity.

I have concluded this wild ride, CALLED LIFE, needs a full fronted aggressive confrontation viewed with open eyes refusing to blame others or situations, institutions we hold no control over and move forward with acceptance based on facts no one can deny.

Looking into myself, I ask the questions.

Where and how?

Thoughts are always just what they are. Internal and hidden. Where do they come from? How are they formed? Are all thoughts from ourselves or are some from an external source? These questions, among so many others, seem to be an important part of life or maybe a teasing side effect on the fringes? Either way the mystery remains untarnished. No proof exists. The answers are elusive, while the facts are clear. The mind contains a strong power over emotions with an ability to cause actions. Good or bad, kind or cruel.

A significant quandary.

Pondering mysteries can be a slippery slope, so I am focused on shifting my stance to produce mental equilibrium.

As a biological creature I need to find a place to walk a straight line, stand firm and balanced. I have chosen a few things to assist me in this endeavor. I mentioned several before. Eating better, slower with less intake, sleeping with consistency and exercise. The exercise side is still a strange new ritual I am fighting with and know I need to continue to wrestle my will toward the value in getting my heart beating and strengthen my bones and muscles. I admire those faithful workout enthusiasts from a distance. It is a necessary component I need to embrace to come into a place of balance. I just dislike it, so I use my rebellious tendencies with well thought-out excuses, but in the end, I am becoming more submissive to a consistent form of exercise.

I added a regiment of nutritional supplements I concluded, thorough study and investigation, may produce favorable results in bio chemical repair and assistance with the slew of issues tumbling through my brain. It is very hard to quantify if there is any value, as there is no diagnostic test to confirm effectiveness. I am not concerned as the ingredients are vitamin and mineral based instead of chemical.

Lithium Ornate, Taurine, Bio-Buffered C, Bio-Omega-3, Bio-B Complex (Super B) and a high dose of vitamin D. This regiment is easy and fairly inexpensive, with no proof of negative side effects, so I will continue along with my offensive, defensive weapons and life-style changes.

I am walking and living in a healthier balanced place, with a degree of stability with anticipation for longevity.

Time will tell.

My road on my journey from Manic life through Mental break, is a strange path where dead ends and switch back can come from unknown places with no forewarning. I stand aware of the stumbling blocks and triggers which have the ability to take me out at a moment's notice so I hold tight and keep my newly acquired weapons locked and loaded.

A bit preachy.

I cannot help myself so please give me a sliver of grace as I share a final thought.

I believe in a benevolent, engaged, purposeful creator, with super-duper plans and purposes. I trust, with every fiber in my being in a gracious loving creator, who is engaged, daily, hourly, moment by moment, in each and every aspect of EIGHT billion eternal beings on the planet today? I do with my whole heart and in every one of the billions of cells in my being. Do I understand? NO, I don't and I do not need to, I believe. What does the word "BELIEVE," mean?

Ask GOOGLE.

NO ONE can say. This is the greatest unanswered question and a broad place for discovery.

Look and observe. Ask and reason. Spent time outside your comfort zone. I understand it is difficult, trust me I do, but I also believe in the Lord Jesus Christ. The creator of all and all that is. Do not get hung up on sects and doctrines and traditions. One day these dividers will wither away, be gathered up and burned.

We as a race, the human race, whatever the hue of the shell of your body, RED, BROWN, YELLOW, BLACK or WHITE, they are all precious in His sight, appears not to make a real difference, except suffering, judgement, pride, decades lost and confusion outside the "TURN a BLIND EYE" and ask no questions crowd.

Not in the sight of God. All remains observed and all will be revealed.

Our minds, are powerful instruments with many unexplainable attributes. Memories, pleasant or otherwise, producing selfish or selfless acts. Good deeds do not confirm goodness. Motives of the heart will come to light balanced against actions. The unseen will be come into a bright light and every knee will bend to truth.

Not a long sermon.

I want to thank YOU. I do not know YOU, but you have been a real asset in my journey. I appreciate You listening, it means more than I can say.

May God bless YOU!

And may God richly Bless;

The BEAUTIFUL PERFECT SEVEN!!!

Amen.